HELENA MORRISSEY is one of Britain's highest-profile businesswomen. She is renowned for her work on gender equality, and for combining a successful career in the male-dominated world of finance with being a mother of nine. Helena started her career in New York with Schroders before joining Newton in 1994 as a junior fund manager. She was appointed chief executive in 2001, a position she held for fifteen years. In 2017, Helena joined Legal and General to lead a new initiative to engage the nation to invest in its financial future – especially women, who are more vulnerable to financial hardship in later life.

In 2010, Helena founded the 30% Club, which began with the aim of achieving more women on boards and has since broadened its efforts to tackle gender inequality from schoolroom to boardroom. The proportion of female directors on top UK company boards has increased from 12.5% to over 30%, and there are now ten 30% Clubs around the world.

Helena was made a Dame in the Queen's 2017 Birthday Honours list for her work on diversity. She has been named one of *Fortune* Magazine's World's 50 Greatest Leaders and was twice voted one of Bloomberg Market's 50 Most Influential People in Finance globally.

A Cambridge Philosophy graduate, Helena is married to a meditation teacher. Their children (six girls and three boys) are now aged between 9 and 27, and they also have a baby grandson, Julian.

Praise for *A Good Time to Be a Girl*:

'A manifesto for career-minded women'

SARAH BAXTER, *Sunday Times*

'What supplies extra authority is where Morrissey is coming from – someone who has reached the summit and who did so while being mother to nine children. All credit to her. Onwards and upwards'   *Evening Standard*

'Morrissey's tone is helpful in the increasingly irascible debate on gender equality … worth listening to'

Financial Times

'A heartfelt manifesto for a more humane and inclusive form of capitalism'

RUTH SUNDERLAND, *Mail on Sunday*

'Morrissey is a suffragist like Millicent Fawcett, convinced that patient social reform can be brought by good women, and men'   ALLISON PEARSON, *Daily Telegraph*

'She makes a great case for ditching the dither, fixing your eyes on the prize, and asking for help where needed and promotion where desired too ... I loved her positivity and push for collective female focus'

HELEN BROWN, *Daily Mail*

'Morrissey is unusual and her book is essentially about why that is a good thing; why people who don't fit the mould should be valued for that, rather than forced to conform ... a refreshing change from the niggling cult of female self-improvement, which starts from the premise that women are probably doing it all wrong'

GABY HINSLIFF, *Observer*

'*Describe what you can bring to this company.*'

a good
time
to be a
girl

a guide to thriving
at work & living well

helena
morrissey

WILLIAM
COLLINS

William Collins
An imprint of HarperCollins*Publishers*
1 London Bridge Street
London SE1 9GF
www.WilliamCollinsBooks.com

First published in Great Britain by William Collins in 2018
This William Collins paperback edition published in 2018

1

A catalogue record for this book is
available from the British Library

ISBN 978-0-00-824164-3

Printed and bound in Great Britain by
CPI Group (UK) Ltd, Croydon

Illustration and diagram credits: Page iv reproduced by kind permission of PRIVATE EYE
magazine/Will McPhail; 59 from Professional Boards Forum BoardWatch, data provided by
BoardEx and The Female FTSE Board Report; 63 © Punch Limited; 93 courtesy of Credit
Suisse Research Institute; 116–17 from Frank Dobbin and Alexándra Kalev, 'Why Diversity
Programs Fail', Harvard Business Review, July–August 2016, reproduced with permission
from Harvard Business Publishing; 119 with permission from www.alexcartoon.com; 158 AF
archive/Alamy Stock Photo; 264 top adapted from Maslow, A. H., 'A theory of human
motivation', Psychological Review, Vol 50(4), Jul 1943, 370–396; 264 bottom courtesy of the
author; 282 'We Are All Wonder Women' cartoon courtesy Catherine and Sarah Satrun; 284
© 2014 KPMG LLP; © YSC Ltd and courtesy of the 30% Club; 295–6 source: JCQ, 2016

Graphs and illustrations on pages 59, 93, 116–17, 264, 284 and 295–6 by Martin Brown

MIX
Paper from
responsible sources
FSC **FSC™ C007454**
www.fsc.org

This book is produced from independently certified FSC paper
to ensure responsible forest management.

For more information visit: www.harpercollins.co.uk/green

In memory of my wonderful grandmothers,
Irene and Amy, who did not have the opportunities
we have today.

Contents

Preface

It's a good time to be a girl! In all honesty, I don't think I could have written that unequivocally before now. Of course, I've seen real progress for women over my fifty-year lifetime, thirty-year career in a male-dominated industry and twenty-five years of motherhood, beginning with one son and now (a final tally) nine children, six girls and three boys. It's certainly been – increasingly – a *better* time to be a woman. As you read my story I hope you will see much to celebrate about the progress we've already made, and how you can create your own opportunities for success, whatever stage you are at in life. I recognise now that I made some 'lucky' choices along the way; by seeing what works and what doesn't, my hope is that you might leave much less to chance.

But today's opportunity is *so much* greater than the unfinished business of the past – and that's why I've written this book now. Gender equality is a well-worn subject but it is not one we have mastered. Despite the huge body of literature, of advice, and opinion, along with very many campaigns and initiatives, the reality is that still only a small number of women have been making it to the top or feel they are fulfilling their potential. Many more tell me they feel discouraged about their prospects, unfulfilled or conflicted in their multiple roles as mothers or carers with careers. They can't see the linkage between their own reality and gender equality efforts that often seem targeted at a narrow group of white, privileged and highly educated women, rather than at *all* women.

Companies, too, are frustrated by limited progress in the numbers of senior women after many years of feeling they are doing a lot to encourage their female and other 'diverse' talent. Sometimes, the result of all these special programmes has – inadvertently – been to do more harm than good; *difference can seem difficult rather than desirable.*

And yet, I am more optimistic today than ever before. I believe that we – men and women, working together – have an unprecedented opportunity to create a new, more successful, quite different approach, one that will not just create more possibilities for girls, but more choices for boys, too – a bolder approach to gender equality that's not aimed merely at training a few women in working practices that have outlived their usefulness. Those women (and even fewer ethnic minority, gay or disabled people) who have made it to the top today are the exceptions, the ones who have mostly played by the rules of the existing game. We now have the chance to *reinvent the game* – not at the expense of men, but by creating new ways of working and living that fit the world of today and tomorrow, not the past. I have spent years listening and engaging with both women and men who tell me very similar things about the pressures they feel to comply with 'norms' that seem habitual rather than right for anyone, or relevant in a digital age.

It's time to think bigger, to act more boldly and, *with men*, devise new ways of working, living and bringing up families together, as equals. But to make the most of this opportunity we need to *stop* leaning in to old-fashioned business practices, cultures, hierarchies and a division of roles that evolved long before technology, or before many girls had a great education.

Leaning in to the status quo is perpetuating what holds us back. Instead, we need to shape the world we want to see.

You may be dubious. How can we change a system that has been stacked up against women for so long? This book provides some practical suggestions for you now; a great example from the past lies in the true story of how the Women's Tennis Association came about (you may have seen the movie *The Battle of the Sexes*). In 1970, nine courageous women led by Billie Jean King refused to 'lean in' to the US Tennis Association, having discovered that the winner of the US Open's men's tournament would receive *twelve times* the woman champion's prize money. On the face of it, the men running the USTA had *all* the power, the financing and the media on their side.

But the women would not accept what was clearly an outrageous situation (and more extreme than we tend to encounter today, thanks in part to their trail-blazing). They established their own tour, signing on for just one dollar each. As Billie Jean put it, 'We weren't sure about our destiny but we knew it was in our hands for the first time.' That destiny turned out to be just great. The new women's tour soon attracted a sponsor and became the foundation stone of the Women's Tennis Association, which today stages over fifty annual events, including four grand slam tournaments. In 2017, the men's and women's US Open champions both received US$3.7 million in prize money.

This redesigning-the-process approach is what we need today. But most gender equality efforts are far less ambitious. Too often, they are aimed at teaching women (and other 'diverse talent') how to play the existing system better. As a result, women are at best playing catch-up, while often feeling dissatisfied and questioning their choices. More of us are becoming lawyers, accountants and doctors, but in the meantime men are pushing onwards, upwards and outwards, taking more entrepreneurial, higher-risk routes to success. Start-ups run by women, for example, currently account for only 2% of US venture capital firms' investments. Following in men's footsteps, emulating the boys but trailing a few years behind them, is not the answer. *As women, we have our*

*own strengths to offer and today we have a better oppor-
tunity to demonstrate that than ever before.*

What makes me so confident? – and so out of sync with
many commentators, who routinely despair at everything
from President Trump to gender pay gaps and the litany
of revelations about sexual harassment? What about
#MeToo, #TimesUp and, in the UK, the sordid revelations
of sexual harassment at the notorious Presidents Club
dinner? Those unsavoury behaviours had been going on
for years; what's different now is that they are being
exposed and addressed. Look at what happened in the
aftermath of the revelations about long-running sexual
harassment in Hollywood, catalysed by the Harvey
Weinstein allegations. We can understand why those who
suffered did not speak up at the time; they felt alone, the
'system' was omnipotent – but today's social media
enabled them to join forces and change the way this issue
will be seen from now onwards. Leaning in to a corrupt
system may have seemed the 'only' option – now, together,
we can transform that system.

The new opportunity I see arises from the very state of
flux we find ourselves in. Today's upheavals are unsettling
and may even look like setbacks, but they also open the
door to a whole new level of progress. That's not just
wishful thinking. My experiences have shown me that
people become receptive to new ideas at moments of dislocation in a way that's very unlikely in stable times. That's
a rational reaction: when the path is smooth, there is little
incentive to consider a different route, but where there is

turbulence, we need to explore new concepts that might show us a way through.

Today's economic, political and societal challenges are certainly immense, driven largely by technology, which is rapidly undermining traditional power structures, changing the nature of leadership, the future of employment, and threatening our security. There is no playbook to consult. Leaders see the need for new thinking, but are grappling with what that looks like.

This book explains how gender balance is an important part of the solution, not – as so many see it – another problem to solve. If we can connect the two, the prize is very great, for each of us as individuals, for equality and for our ability to solve increasingly complex problems. The stark reality is that if we are going to resolve the big disconnects, we need to re-engineer our collective thinking, and that means involving more women. Feminine traits – empathy, collaborative behaviour, the ability to connect emotionally with those we are seeking to influence – can help us find answers.

Of course, men can have those feminine attributes too; what is important is to move on from the macho command-and-control regime that we have become used to for centuries. People will not be told what to do by leaders who don't connect with them and they don't trust.

So amidst the current upheavals, we have the chance to develop a new, shared understanding of what's needed to be successful, in our family lives as well as our careers; what's needed for men as well as women to have more freedom in how they live and for these positive changes to affect many people. Happily, in my experience many men in many countries around the world now want gender equality too – and that's key to consigning the whole topic to the history books. Short of a revolution, people on the outside need those on the inside to help them progress. 'He for she' (and 'she for he') is the right approach.

I have seen change happen once many people start to share the desire to reach a certain outcome, and then work together towards it. A multitude of individuals taking small steps together in the same direction creates a powerful momentum.

So what happens next is very much up to all of us – and that includes you. You don't need to choose between focusing on your own career and creating the conditions for broader progress; increasingly, those goals are linked. We can write our own story, individually and collectively. This book will show you how to make the most of today's new opportunities, whether you are still at school, starting out in your working life, looking to progress at mid-career or already at a senior level, whether you are a daughter, son, parent, mentor, mentee, teacher, pupil, CEO or apprentice. First, you need an open mind; much of the current thinking around diversity is – ironically – encouraging the exact opposite. The diversity agenda has been hijacked by virtue signallers, with universities leading the way in shutting down freedom of expression in the name of 'inclusion' (*sic*). A diverse society needs diverse thinking, especially around how we create *real* inclusion, yet it has become heretical to question ineffective approaches. If we're going to make real progress, we first need a licence to challenge what has clearly not been working.

I'm certainly not complacent. In my own lifetime I have already seen many stops and starts in the journey towards gender equality and of course there were very many years of effort long before, including the sacrifices made by women who had to fight hard for the right to vote a century ago. Even since I started writing this book a number of critical developments have occurred – and will continue to occur – because great change involves challenging episodes, lurches forward, steps back and the inevitable sense that we are faltering. But this is a necessary part of the process.

And today's great opportunity is far from universal, with terrible atrocities against women and girls even on our own doorsteps: in England, a case of female genital mutilation (FGM) is discovered or treated every hour and child trafficking referrals (often involving girls for sexual abuse) hit a record high in 2017. Even equality for many will be a hollow victory if these crimes continue. We must also ensure that white, disadvantaged young men, who now have the lowest educational attainment levels of any group, aren't left behind as we push on towards a world of greater opportunity for bright young women.

These are real challenges but they remind us of the need to improve the whole, not just the outcomes for a few. I am excited about exploring new ways of working that will enable more women to fulfil their potential, more men to play a greater role in their children's lives, better thinking to solve today's problems and broader definitions of success. A time when my six daughters not only can be but need to be themselves and when my sons have more choices than their father's generation, too. A time when, as Lord Browne, former CEO of BP, who came out as gay after forty-one years in business, says, 'women don't have to be honorary men, blacks honorary whites, gays honorary straights'.

At which point, we'll look back and wonder how we got so accustomed to anything else.

Chapter 1

A tale of two career women

Keep away from people who try to belittle your ambitions. Small people always do that, but the really great make you feel that you, too, can become great.

MARK TWAIN

Consider two real-life career stories. The first involves a 26-year-old British woman who has just returned to her role as a fund manager at a prestigious City firm after five months' maternity leave. She has worked for the company for five years, having joined its graduate training scheme straight after university. Over 1,500 applications were received for just twenty graduate places. A few days into the training programme, she was selected for a two-year apprenticeship in New York, working for one of the firm's top global bond fund managers. A promising start to her career.

She found New York both daunting (it was the first time she had ever travelled beyond Europe) and exciting. The work was intensive and the hours long but she enjoyed learning new skills and was soon given more responsibility. As she thought about her future, she found it encouraging that two impressive American women in their forties were leading the firm's rapid local growth.

When the young woman returned to London, she found the office environment markedly different. The pace was much slower – the daily morning meeting started at 11.45 a.m. – and she was the only woman in a team of 16. Still, the work was interesting and there was plenty of it. She was always first to arrive in the office each day, to deal with queries from Japanese clients in their time zone.

The firm made its annual promotions each April. The goal for high-flying graduates was to be promoted to manager level after five years – coinciding almost exactly with the woman's return from her first maternity leave. Her two male contemporaries received the promotion. She did not. Disappointed, she asked where she needed to improve but the answer came back, 'Your work is great, there's just some doubt over your commitment with a baby.' Shocked, she struggled to accept that her promising career had fizzled out so quickly.

Our second story concerns a woman nearly a decade older, the mother of five children. The youngest three have just celebrated their first, second and third birthdays. She also works as a fund manager in the City, for a less well known, much smaller firm. She joined seven years ago, as number two (out of two) on the bond desk, a junior role in a relatively backwater area for the company. On the face of it, a less promising situation than the younger woman's original circumstances.

This story has a happier outcome, though, because the 35-year-old with five young children and just seven years' service is suddenly – and quite unexpectedly – appointed chief executive officer following a takeover of the company. Over the next 15 years, the new CEO and her colleagues will grow assets under management from £20 billion to over £50 billion, develop a number of market-leading strategies and a strong reputation. She will also go on to have four more children – yes, nine in total.

One a tale of unexpected disappointment, the other of perhaps equally surprising success. Yet both stories are actually about the same woman – me.

So how did I fail to reach even the first rung on the corporate ladder at one firm, yet become chief executive in just seven years at another? Three factors created a formula for success.

The initial setback certainly taught me to do things quite differently the second time around. When I started working in 1987 I genuinely believed that hard work and aptitude determined how far anyone could progress. It simply did not occur to me then that the masculine dress code adopted by many career women at the time (big shoulder-padded suits) suggested that it was still very much a man's world.

And of course my early experiences of working life had been unusually exciting for a graduate trainee, glamorous even, and that had made me quickly feel confident. The first *Wall Street* movie was released just after I moved to New York, as was *Working Girl*. The environment was energising. The two women I saw at the top, seemingly in control of their own destiny, distracted me from the reality that they were anomalous and had made either hard choices or sacrifices to get to the top. They travelled extensively and had limited time for their personal lives. Both married late: one was childless, the other underwent (well-publicised) fertility treatment to finally conceive her only child. While these women looked like wonderful role models in terms of career achievements, their lives certainly did not appeal to everyone.

The London office was very different to New York, yet I had no inkling of how my maternity would be perceived. I hadn't given any indication that I was less ambitious or committed either during my pregnancy or after my return. When the list of promotions came around and my name wasn't on it, I genuinely thought there was something I hadn't been doing well, that I could improve for next time. When my boss made it so clear, in a way that wouldn't happen today, I was disappointed and surprised but at least I knew where I stood. My first reaction was confusion – I simply hadn't made the connection between being a new mother and failing to get that promotion. There was then a moment of clarity: I could not change my existing environment, so I had to find a new one.

The whole episode was a valuable career lesson. It taught me the need to be resilient, which has been so important in many situations – but not to be immutable, not to bounce back from the disappointment only to take another blow. When I started at the next firm, Newton Investment Management, I knew that I needed to take responsibility for my career. I needed to strategise more, not just wait for my contribution to be recognised.

During the recruitment process I had been interviewed by the firm's founder, Stewart Newton. It was an encouraging sign, that someone so senior was involved in hiring someone so junior. Stewart was fascinating to talk to, he loved the bond and currency markets, was animated and probing and always on the lookout for investment talent. Towards the end of my first year, my (female) boss resigned and Stewart told me that he would hire a 'bond guru' to lead the area. I took a deep breath and asked if I might look after the portfolios in the meantime. Stewart agreed, with a few reasonable conditions. I would have to sit next to him and each afternoon we would meet in his office towards the end of the day to go over my trades and ideas. Effectively, and unofficially, he became my mentor, and the arrangement helped me to learn from him while he grew more confident in my abilities.

Stewart liked to move around the office, changing his seat every six weeks or so to oversee different areas of the investment team. I therefore had to move too, which seemed slightly embarrassing at the time but helped me to get to know my colleagues. The experience of speaking up and then being given the portfolios to manage encouraged me to seek other opportunities. I quickly realised that if I asked, the answer was usually 'yes', as long as I was making a reasonable request, had something to offer and was performing well. When interesting committees were formed and I wasn't included, I asked for a seat at the table. I always phrased my requests constructively: 'Oh, I wonder if I might join the economics group? Perhaps I could contribute the bond analysis and it would be useful for me to hear what else is being considered.' There was no confrontation, no argument, and the door usually opened. Inevitably, there were setbacks, but I tried to learn and to see past them, with my recovery from that earlier disappointment encouraging me to persevere. (For the record, I have always struggled with negative feedback, finding it hard not to take criticism personally, and I've noticed this in other women too – although it may be that men are just better at disguising their feelings. We shall return to the subject later.) And while I sought opportunities to be heard, I stayed focused on performing well since that was the best advert for my capabilities.

I also looked to build my reputation in the marketplace. When I had been looking for that second job, it was harder than it needed to have been because I hadn't built a network. I found that it was actually quite easy to be noticed as a young woman running bond funds. One year I was shortlisted for a 'Fund manager of the year' award and the other nominees were not just all men, but all called Paul. I did win, and I'd like to think it wasn't just because I was the only one who could be easily identified, but I'll never be quite sure. When the three Pauls and I were panellists together at investment conferences, the moderators would usually give me more airtime. There were advantages, but it was obvious that the few women who were making it through in my own industry were part of a very male-dominated club.

Two other critical factors helped me to progress so far and so quickly at Newton. I was working for a company where results were what mattered, and my husband Richard and I had developed a real partnership to care and provide for our family. Together with my newfound career awareness, this was a powerful combination, but by no means complex or mysterious.

The first company I had worked for was very traditional at the time, like most long-established City of London institutions. Founded in 1804 it was built on literally centuries-old practices that revolved around how men habitually liked to work. The atmosphere was 'clubby'. There was a daily reminder of the hierarchy: each afternoon, a uniformed butler wheeled a trolley round the floor and served tea and biscuits to those of associate director or higher rank. Members of the asset allocation committee, the most senior group of investors, had typically served twenty years or more at the company. We would be asked to submit papers from time to time but weren't invited to participate in their meetings. The structure was rigid and junior staff needed to fit in if they were to progress. While the New York office had its own more energetic and youthful culture, the London headquarters was the epicentre of power.

In contrast, there was a friendly, collegiate atmosphere at Newton. The very first week I joined, people asked for my opinion. If anyone had anything worthwhile to contribute, they would have the opportunity. The company didn't really have a formal structure, more a fluid process built around the goal of delivering strong investment performance, with no one really paying much attention to status or tenure. My job interview with Stewart was not unusual; he took a great interest in hiring anyone who was going to be part of the investment team, however lowly. He made a point of frequently emphasising that the firm was a meritocracy and encouraged me to be my own character, which helped me to grow in confidence. I became increasingly bold in my investment views, but also more comfortable in being fully myself. I dressed more distinctively, and colleagues began to ask me to represent the firm to clients or at conferences. As expectations increased, even though I had inevitable moments of self-doubt, I rose to meet the next level of challenge. Partly, this was due to necessity: in this early phase of my time at Newton, Richard was made redundant and although he found another job in due course, I was spurred on by the responsibility of providing for our family. Yet persevering didn't feel like an uphill struggle.

The qualities of the firm that enabled me to thrive weren't the result of any diversity initiative but *intrinsic* to its everyday culture.

When I eventually left Newton after more than twenty years, my very first consideration when weighing up future opportunities was corporate culture. Did a potential employer welcome diverse opinions and encourage staff to express views that might differ from the consensus (or the boss); was there *evidence* of a meritocracy? I quickly turned down even interesting-sounding roles if it was also clear that the firm was rigidly command-and-control. By now I knew that a truly *inclusive* culture was essential if I was going to be able to really contribute, to be successful and happy. My new firm, Legal and General, didn't just tick theoretical boxes; I had worked with enough people there (both senior and less so) on a variety of industry-wide projects to know we were a good fit.

Corporate culture has been in the spotlight since the 2008 financial crisis, with a number of scandals showing how poor behaviours can have disastrous consequences, destroying reputations and share prices. Culture, the social and psychological character of a firm, can seem a nebulous concept and it can be difficult to judge from the outside, especially since most mid-sized and large companies now make all the right statements about diversity and inclusion. The question is whether these statements are embedded in day-to-day behaviours.

A short while ago a woman approached me in the gym, seeking my advice. She was struggling to live up to what she felt was expected at the investment firm where she worked. I know the chief executive quite well and believe that he really wants women to thrive at the company. A few years ago he called me to ask how to attract more female graduates (at the time only10% of their applicants were women). He has been genuinely supportive of broader efforts to improve diversity in the currently very white, very middle-class and male-dominated fund management industry. Yet the woman's experience was discouraging; the mother of two young children, she had been assured at the interviews that her role did not involve much travel. In fact, soon after joining she had been sent on four long-haul trips in quick succession. Another trip was looming the following week. The travel was taking its toll on both her family and her day-to-day work: worried that she was falling behind, she had gone into the office at the weekend to catch up, only to find many colleagues there. The family-friendly talk had proved just that.

I advised her to talk to her manager, to calmly explain that she was keen to work hard but the current situation was unsustainable – and to give specific examples. My suspicion was that no one had intentionally misled her, that they simply hadn't joined the dots between what had been said and what was transpiring in practice (not an excuse, but often the reality). She may well have said yes to the first trip thinking it was a one-off, made a success of it and then been an obvious choice for further travel, with the interview fading from everyone's consciousness except her own. The likelihood was that her manager would much rather adapt than see her resign.

A lack of consistency between what is said and what is done is a common but significant problem. It breeds disillusionment and distrust. Leadership teams are often very keen, almost desperate to see a better gender mix and frustrated by a lack of progress but completely oblivious to situations like my gym companion's. If we don't speak up – not belligerently or militantly, but to point out the inconsistencies – the gap in their understanding will persist. Of course, some jobs necessitate travel and episodes of working round-the-clock, but constant pressure should not be a role requirement: it certainly does not bring out the best in anyone, man or woman, and is unsustainable.

This example highlights a widespread problem: *diversity and inclusion are usually treated as enhancements, not as core to business success*. There are still many challenges to the idea that diversity does enhance results, and we will examine the evidence later, but for now let's explore why there is such a prevalent gap between what is said by CEOs and what happens in practice.

Dame Fiona Woolf hosted a diversity conference at the Mansion House when she was Lord Mayor of the City of London in 2015 (only the second female Lord Mayor in 800 years). I was keen to speak at this particular conference because the target audience was middle managers, often thought to be the sticking point when it comes to making progress towards more inclusive workplace cultures. After my presentation one gentleman raised his hand. How, he wanted to know, did we fit diversity and inclusion into our already busy work schedules? He wondered if I recommended allocating specific time to the issue, say, an hour a week? He couldn't see that this was like suggesting we allocate a time to say, being nice.

That may sound like an outlier but this lack of understanding is not uncommon. One of the reasons why we have made relatively slow progress is our tendency to separate 'diversity and inclusion' efforts into a distinct area. Instead, they should be inseparable aspects of culture. Attitudes and behaviours are hard to change, but we can shake them up by making the issue central, as part of the everyday.

If you run a business, you may think you are already approaching diversity in this integrated, seamless way. One idea to test that out: are jobs at your company flexible by default or do staff need to request permission to work in a flexible or agile way? In 2015, PriceWaterhouseCoopers in Australia took what might seem a radical step, to make *all* its 6,000 roles flexible, giving employees the freedom to choose their own working hours. Staff might work part-time, job-share, vary their work hours or work remotely. They didn't need to make their case: instead, their manager was responsible for piecing together different working practices to ensure that the team was effective. For most people, it wasn't a question of working either more or fewer hours, just differently. Significantly, the motivation behind PwC's move was to attract high calibre talent to the firm.

At Newton, in something of an experiment soon after becoming CEO, I introduced a four-day-week option for any member of staff who wished to take it. The option was for an initial six months, and then employees could decide to stay on the four-day week or revert to full time. As many men as women took up the offer, including some of the most senior male fund managers, who then stayed with this arrangement for a decade or more. There was no stigma attached to the decision and it was not a diversity initiative but part of overall talent motivation efforts and management of the company's resources. At the same time, the scheme certainly helped maternity returners feel confident that they would still be valued if they wanted to work a shorter week – and that they wouldn't be perceived as getting 'special treatment'.

In 2012, I helped devise a national survey of women's experiences in the workplace, led by Business in the Community, one of the Prince of Wales' charities. We wanted to hear particularly from women in the 28–40 age group since that is when women's career paths tend to fall behind those of their male colleagues (and no, it's not just because that's when women have children – the data shows that women with no children also tend to be promoted less than men). A total of 25,000 people took part in Project 28–40, including women older and younger than our target group, and 2,000 men, giving useful reference points. The feedback showed that only half the women felt supported by their employer in their career aspirations. Flexible working was seen as helping with work–life balance but there was a stigma attached, undermining chances of career progression. Only 40% of respondents said that their organisation valued flexible working as a way of *working efficiently*.

Overwhelmingly, women said they did not want special programmes, they just wanted to be managed better.

Increasingly, in our knowledge-based economy, performance will be measurable in terms of results, rather than hours at the desk. Some jobs lend themselves more easily to this and, given that flexible working was not even a concept in the late 1980s, I made a fortunate choice of career. At the end of each quarter or year, the performance of the funds I managed stood as an objective record for anyone to see. It would have been much tougher to combine a large family with being, say, a corporate finance lawyer, where the work is transaction-based and individual contributions are often measured in billable hours. In 2016, PwC's 25th annual Law Firms Survey revealed that newly qualified lawyers at the UK's top ten law firms are set an average annual billing target of nearly 1,600 hours. Perhaps unsurprisingly, most lawyers fall short.

The meritocracy that I benefited from at Newton *can* be the corporate cultural norm, not the exception. Beyond a small number of organisations, we haven't yet really shaken up our working structures to attract more diverse talent – or taken full advantage of technology to make work more of an activity than a place. Instead, we've tended to add in programmes around the edges designed to encourage those who are outside the 'norm', but often this draws attention to the problem and may have the counterproductive effect of making difference appear troublesome. We'll explore approaches that work better in Chapter 6.

There's also a tendency to leave those in the diverse or under-represented groups in charge of solving the problem of their own under-representation. This is, I promise, an impossible task (even if an executive sponsor is drafted in to cheerlead). 'Affinity groups' or special interest networks can encourage people to feel less alone, but won't do much for their chances of promotion and obviously do not foster inclusion. Talking to ourselves is never going to get us very far.

One evening, I arrived to give a speech at a diversity event hosted by one of the big four accountancy firms. The first problem was that I could see from a quick glance that the audience comprised only women, ethnic minorities, and one or two disabled people – where were all the white men? I was told they hadn't been invited, which immediately seemed to limit the event's potential impact. The few members of the leadership team who were there in a supportive role appeared downcast. I asked what the problem was: earlier that same day, the firm had the chance to pitch to an important prospect but the presentation team had been asked to leave as soon as they entered the room. Apparently the potential client had specifically asked for a diverse team but the group that had arrived to present was all-white, male and middle-aged. My hosts explained that of course they had read the brief, and a young woman had been due to go along but she was off sick and no one had remembered the diversity point until it was too late. The issue just wasn't front and centre of anyone's mind. In contrast, Stewart Newton had created an investment philosophy where difference was integral to the thought-process, where multiple perspectives were valued. That was great not just for me, but for anyone who enjoyed thinking laterally, being challenged and challenging others.

The third essential ingredient behind my newfound career success was the true partnership with Richard. My career setback after our first son was born had not put us off having more children. Both Richard and I had grown up in small families and shared a romantic vision of the happy chaos of a large number of children. When we married we said we would love to have five. Neither of us is from a wealthy background and we had to be self-sufficient. Fulfilling our dream of a big and happy family involved some stresses, including financially, although we were conscious that this was our choice.

We had not planned to start our family so quickly, but were young, rather relaxed and, as it turned out, able to produce babies rather easily (or, at least, conceive). Our first child, Fitzroy, was born ten months after our wedding. Young women often ask me when is a 'good' time to have a baby. I always say there is no ideal time, although I am grateful that we started to have our children when we were young by today's standards. We weren't perhaps ready, but as first-time parents do, we learned quickly.

The financial struggles when Fitz was born were challenging, though. We were amongst the many young professionals who had borrowed money in the late 1980s to buy a small flat, only to see interest rates soar and our mortgage payments balloon, while property prices collapsed. Neither of us had a high salary and for a while, our outgoings outstripped our earnings, a clearly unsustainable situation. One income was not enough to cover the mortgage so we both needed to work full-time, but our only realistic childcare option was a day nursery near my office. The nursery fees were around a quarter of our after-tax income before we had paid even a penny of the outsized mortgage bill. That first year I returned to work after having Fitz was tough, particularly when I didn't get the promotion that might have eased our financial strain, but the experience also made us very determined. My new job at Newton came with a salary rise and Richard found a higher-paid position too. Mortgage rates came down and although our flat was worth far less than we had paid for it, bigger properties had suffered even larger price falls, so we were finally able to move.

Buying a modest house enabled us to hire a wonderful nanny, Paula, who stayed with us for more than twenty years. She always lived out, which gave us precious family time together and space for her, but meant that either Richard or I had to be home before she left at 6 p.m. Richard was a financial journalist and had multiple daily deadlines so I would always do the morning shift, waiting until she arrived at 7.30 a.m. Paula was incredibly reliable, but every day I felt anxious about getting to the office on time by public transport.

There was no slack at all in the arrangement, no room for error or lateness, and the stress of us both rushing in and out of the home, often distracted by work when we were there, trying to 'do it all', was taking its toll, including on our relationship. Richard and I needed to work out how not just to survive but to be happy. We took our time having our second and third children, who were born more than three years apart.

It is a big part of our story that when we were expecting Millie, our fourth, who was born just a year after our third child, both Richard and I knew something had to change. With another baby on the way we felt at breaking point and one evening discussed how we could possibly make it all work. Richard volunteered to go freelance and work from home: he would be able to play a bigger role in bringing up our family. He also wanted a freer existence, having never enjoyed office politics. Over time, as we had yet more children, his opportunity (and desire) to take on paid work dwindled and he became a full-time, stay-at-home dad.

This reversal of traditional roles was ahead of its time: Millie is now at university. It has not always been perfect (nothing is) but it has been key to our ultimately happy family life as well as helping my career. At the beginning, we were completely open as to how things might evolve – neither of us knew whether we would be able to afford the arrangement becoming permanent. We definitely had to be careful about money: 'staycations', for example, were a necessity rather than a choice and it was a long time before we could decorate our new home. These were minor sacrifices for our happier family life.

Both of us feel confident that the set-up has been beneficial to the children: Richard enjoys being at home, is completely dedicated to being at every sports fixture, likes cooking and (most of the time) doesn't mind the endless chauffeuring. It's been wonderful for me to know that the children have been benefiting, both logistically and emotionally, from one parent being at home. Meanwhile, since I have always wanted to be home whenever possible, throughout my career I have been disciplined about leaving the office in time for family suppers most evenings. This time together at the end of each day has always been an important part of our family life.

Of course, with nine children, it would have been impossible for me to get to all (or even most) of the school plays, concerts and ballet performances, so I have prioritised those events that are each child's 'special' thing. I do regret missing certain moments, especially not being there when someone simply wants to talk, but I know it has been a good arrangement overall. We cannot attain perfection, and to strive for it is a recipe for feeling inadequate. Most importantly, our children are happy and thriving (at least most of them, most of the time). Some of my male peers never see their children during the week – a situation that would make both my family and me quite miserable.

Ours is still an unusual arrangement and I often get asked about it, including questions about whether I feel guilty (not exactly helpful at those moments when I do) and how I 'have it all'. When I guest-edited BBC Radio 4's

Today programme in December 2016, I asked five high-powered men, ranging from bestselling author Michael Lewis to the chairman of Barclays Bank, John Mcfarlane, how they balanced work and family life. All of them said it was a question they had never been asked before. It was also interesting that none of them answered that it was all possible thanks to their wonderful wife or partner. I suspect this was for fear of seeming politically incorrect, although I feel completely able to credit Richard for making it all possible, and he is praised for his modernity.

I realise now that the conversation Richard and I had all those years ago about how, together, we could make it all work is still quite uncommon. It's a very personal matter for each family to work out how to bring up children with love and time, how to earn enough money, develop careers, contribute to the community and, hopefully, have time for wider family, friends and fun. Working together to make things as good as they can be, whatever role each of us plays, is crucial to building a happy life together. When she was CEO of the *Financial Times*, Rona Fairhead was asked for one piece of advice for girls. 'Marry well,' she said, before explaining that she didn't mean marry someone wealthy, but someone who understands you, who is a genuine partner.

We do not always have the luxury of choice and I am very conscious that not everyone can find a true partner in life. Sheryl Sandberg tragically became a single mother when her 47-year-old husband died suddenly: she has since spoken poignantly of her awareness that the chapter entitled 'Make your partner a real partner' in her influential book *Lean In* does not always apply. (Sandberg also realised through her terrible loss that it is very hard to 'lean in' when life is difficult; in her own words, 'Lean in? I could barely stand up').

Young women sometimes say it is easy for me, with Richard's support, a relatively high salary and greater flexibility with my time than someone starting out. I always stress that while I'm very aware of these advantages, they haven't always been there. Struggles have been part of not just my journey but most people's too; it's almost inevitable that any successful person has had their share of failures. When Richard and I hit our low point of financial stress, my mother reminded me that nothing lasts for ever, and that helped me to focus on finding a solution rather than be dragged down by anxiety. The experience again made me realise that I could not rely too much on others but needed to take control of my own destiny as far as possible. We will return to these big topics later; for now, let me emphasise the importance of recognising that each of our lives is different, but there are things we can do that will make the most of a situation – or shrink our opportunities. Whether you have a partner or not, you need a few strong allies, friends, mentors: people you can really confide in, who will give you good advice. Ultimately we have to make our own decisions, but no person is an island and none of us has an unlimited well of confidence, or all the answers.

I was once interviewed on live TV about workplace equality and the (female) presenter kept challenging me on one point: surely, she argued, it must be possible for both partners to have 'high-powered' careers with children? It was slightly perplexing that she kept returning to the topic, but as I walked off set, the producer explained that my interviewer was getting married very soon. Apparently, she and her fiancé were struggling with the idea that one of them might need to be less focused on their career once they started a family. Both saw that as a potential career setback or even a death knell – and the woman was particularly worried because she could see it would be more likely to be her, not her future husband, stepping back. Looking ahead, I am confident that more people (not just women) will be able to take advantage of more fluid ways of working, to 'dial up' or 'dial down' their careers from time to time – and so feel less concerned about making a binary choice. As life expectancy increases, we will need to work longer and may have two or three careers (this may be forced upon us, as employment opportunities change along with the rise of artificial intelligence). Taking a few years off in the middle, or changing the pace for a while, should really make little difference overall. 'Returnships' – the opportunity to return to a meaningful role after a gap of several years – are likely to become increasingly prevalent and part of a big shake-up in employment patterns.

For all the discussion about women and our changing role in society, there tends to be little focus on what this means for men. Richard has always maintained that the logical extension of all the efforts to help women fulfil their career potential is for men to have more choices too. Gender equality cuts both ways and redefining what success means for all of us is part of what we need to do. There are, today, still quite straitjacketed expectations about what it is to be a successful man. As he made the transition to full-time parent, Richard became frustrated by the question 'What do you do?' – it was so clear that men are largely defined by their job. His honest answer would leave people hesitating about what to say next and they often seemed embarrassed. So he experimented with various ways of explaining his role, including referring to his other interests, such as painting, meditation and spiritual healing. We are still a long way from the point where having a stay-at-home father is seen as just as normal for families as a stay-at-home mother. (Or where a man can praise his wife for being a wonderful stay-at-home mother just as I can praise Richard today.)

Those factors that made all the difference to my career – self-awareness, meritocracy, and a supportive partner – are, I believe, very relevant to young, ambitious women – and men – today. My story is not a template, however. There is now much greater scope to be different and to influence your own path than there was thirty, twenty or even ten years ago. Women of my age (or a decade older or younger) in senior roles today are the exception, not the norm. We have been allowed into a masculine club at the top of business or politics. I think of us as a 'transition' generation, benefiting from the work that so many generations of women did before us, but still needing to mostly fit in with the status quo. Young people have different challenges, with uncertainty over employment prospects affecting both boys and girls. But they also have a greater opportunity to bring their differences into the workplace right from the start, to help create paths towards new thinking, new solutions to today's challenges, not more of the same.

Chapter 2

New leadership required

We can't solve problems with the same kind of thinking we used when we created them.

ALBERT EINSTEIN

While my career had been progressing well at Newton, the opportunity to become chief executive just seven years after joining was unexpected – most of all by me. The takeover of the firm by Mellon Bank, an American company, had been long planned and took several years to complete. It seemed probable that some members of the management team might decide to move on. As part of the four-strong Investment Strategy group, I was a potential candidate for the role of chief investment officer (CIO). I was keen to get the job if it became available – I loved making the big strategic investment calls, enjoyed life at Newton and got on well with my colleagues. I was feeling restricted by my existing role: at the time, one piece of US economic data was driving bond markets around the world – the employment figures released the first Friday of each month. My whole working life revolved around this data point. In particular, one long weekend sticks in my memory. My husband and I had taken our children to visit their grandparents and instead of enjoying our family time I was glued to the news. The data was much stronger than anticipated, my positioning was all wrong and I felt distraught, helpless and rubbish at my job. This was obviously an overreaction, and as Richard and I discussed my loss of perspective, it was clear that I needed a new, broader challenge.

So I was delighted when Mellon's UK-based chief offered me the CIO role, which offered the opportunity to lead a talented team, as well as to expand my horizons. My new boss told me that he would fill the other vacancy himself, adding the Newton CEO position to his responsibilities. Next morning, one of my colleagues stopped by my desk and quietly mentioned that the other senior investors had met and unfortunately they didn't want me to become the CIO. Taken aback, having thought I had their support, I asked if they would meet me to explain why. As we went into the room, I mentally ran through my options, realising that I would probably have to leave, given what seemed (to me) to be a vote of no confidence.

It turned out that my colleagues thought, reasonably, that it was important for the CIO to have an equities background since most of the firm's assets were invested in the stock market. The conversation turned to my leadership skills, and there it was clear that I did have a following. Before I knew it, the suggestion was being made that I become the chief executive officer instead.

My first reaction was a sense of relief. I loved working at Newton and didn't want to leave. I also knew this meant that it was in relation to the specific role that my ability was in doubt rather than an objection to me as a person. At the same time, I was disoriented by what had just happened. We all left the room and I ducked into an adjacent one and gathered my thoughts. I called my husband and told him 'I'm not going to be the CIO any more, I'm going to be the CEO.' 'What does that entail?' he asked and I answered, truthfully, 'I have no idea.' What I did know was that I believed in what Newton had to offer our clients, in the team and the process, that I could lead and that this was an unusual, perhaps once-in-a-lifetime opportunity.

It was never articulated in these precise terms but I believe one reason why colleagues were prepared to back me as CEO was because of my collaborative style of leadership. We obviously faced a number of challenges immediately following the takeover, and my first task was to rebuild confidence. Where there was a problem, it was my job to come up with a solution. While I certainly didn't have all the answers and frequently needed the input of colleagues, I had a clear sense of what we were trying to achieve.

I've often reflected on that bizarre day. I was only 35 and had no business experience or management training. The firm managed some £20 billion of assets. I had no real idea of how challenging the next few years would be – but also how fulfilling it would be to eventually come out the other side, when we had – together – achieved real progress as a company. I realise now that the decision to say yes rather than what might have seemed a more sensible no to the CEO role, was, in fact, the making of my career. *A moment of disruption was my great opportunity.*

That experience, particularly in those early years, taught me the importance of focusing on long-term goals, rather than on all the steps we can't see clearly in the moment but know we need to take to get there. A bridge will often open up when we get stranded, as long as we don't get distracted or lose sight of that end goal. My six daughters have heard me tell them to 'leap before you look' so many times that they now chant it whenever one sister is dithering, but all too often I have seen women (more than men) focus more on what might go wrong than on the prospect of success. We'll return to this in Chapter 7 – it is vital to recognise and counteract this tendency to hold ourselves back if we're to be able to capitalise on the opportunities ahead of us right now.

As a novice CEO (and frankly also when experienced) I made many mistakes. Just one day into my new role, I took a call from a tabloid newspaper. I had never had any media training and this was long before companies had 'corporate communications' teams. The journalist asked sensible questions about my vision for Newton, which I answered tentatively. She then probed into my family life. Here I felt on firmer footing and happily obliged with some candid information and thoughts on combining family and career. The next morning everyone was very quiet in the office and when I asked if all was OK, a copy of the paper was handed across. There was a rather sensational story on page three entitled 'Billion Dollar Babe', describing me as 'the pinstripes' pinup'. Richard correctly pointed out that those descriptions were wholly inaccurate (my comment at the end that 'five [children] is plenty' has also come back to haunt me), but I felt embarrassed and frivolous for contributing to the piece. After that experience, I didn't talk to the press for several years and only agreed to do interviews again when I wanted to draw attention to the issue of women in the workplace.

I can see now that in the broader scheme of things that silly newspaper article was not a big deal, but at the time everything felt magnified. The whole experience of my early days as a CEO was a very steep learning curve, with many moments of self-doubt before I emerged on the other side, older, wiser and just possibly better at my job than if I had taken a more conventional route to get there, if only because I had to learn so quickly.

Happily, I did make a few good calls in those early days. One was to shut out the siren voices telling me to reinvent Newton, to develop new strategies that weren't core to our strengths. I had already learned – in life as well as at work – that we cannot always please everyone and that it's a mistake even to try. In business, the key is to offer *something* of value to some people; in life, to know what matters to you, a framework for the myriad decisions each of us needs to take. At that moment at Newton, it was more important than ever to focus on what we did best, to ensure our clients were being well served and that they had confidence in us to continue performing. We were not static, however, the marketplace was changing around us so we consciously evolved our investment services rather than sticking rigidly to what had worked in the past. As author, analyst and former trader Nassim Nicholas Taleb puts it, we were 'antifragile', seeking opportunity from change. At the same time, I needed to nurture the culture that had been so central to the business since it was founded. I was merely (and just about) first amongst equals, carrying the ultimate responsibility but in no way superior to my talented colleagues.

Different situations require different leadership styles and while my approach may not be the right one for every scenario or every company, it worked well for Newton at the time. There had been a dislocation, and a collaborative approach enabled our employees, the firm's key asset, to contribute to the vision of our future.

This all happened a long time ago; now we can see a much more widespread desire for 'alternative' forms of political and business leadership. The command-and-control approach that has prevailed for very many years, where a narrow elite tells other people what to do, is rapidly becoming ineffective in a networked world. There is much less deference to those in official leadership roles; leaders need to *merit* their authority. So the role is less about sitting at the top of a pyramid and giving orders, more about positioning oneself at the centre of influence. I felt this acutely as Newton's new CEO: one minute I was one of many fund managers, the next I was officially the boss, but not in a position to *instruct* my colleagues. Instead, my role was to lead by influencing them, having first listened to what was on their minds, then to form a plan that took account of their views (or explain why I was going in a different direction), and bring them with me. This was partly the result of the circumstances of my appointment but it's also a feature of active investment management firms, since talented investors often see themselves as self-employable. The CEO is more akin to the conductor of an orchestra than a prima donna. This leadership model is becoming the reality for many other industries, and in politics too.

Many people see the shock events of 2016 – most notably Brexit and the election of President Trump – as setbacks for diversity. Of course, at the time no one asked voters to indicate the reasons *why* they voted the way they did, and all sorts of interpretations can be offered. In my view, while the specific reasons vary, the fact that in both the UK and the US many people voted *against* the establishment is key. The shocks themselves demonstrate how power is changing in a way that *should be* good news for democracy and equality. *People will no longer be told what to do by leaders who don't connect with them.* The problem is, if this isn't recognised and addressed, the protests morph into extremism.

I was flying back from a business trip in Denver on the evening of the UK's EU referendum in June 2016. As we landed, everyone checked their phones for the result and an American lady tapped me on the shoulder; 'It was Remain, right?' 'No actually, Leave won,' I replied. She looked perplexed and exclaimed, genuinely shocked, 'But we sent the President!' She couldn't see that this might have been a counterproductive move: the Americans 'sent the President'; the British government dropped Remain leaflets on doorsteps, and people voted the exact opposite. In the US presidential election, it wasn't enough of a change that Hillary Clinton was the first female nominee; she was also perceived as part of the establishment, as likely to maintain the status quo. Donald Trump's comments make many of us wince, but during the election campaign, he reached out to those voters who were certainly not living the 'American dream', who had not participated in economic or income growth, who felt that no one was listening or cared – and he connected with them.

We have seen the desire for change many times before, of course, but technology makes it much more likely to be fulfilled. We now have an (almost) level playing field in our access to vast amounts of instant information. Anyone with a network and something interesting to say can influence others through social media, without any formal authority. And anything and everything is discoverable, exposing the humanity of leaders. There needs to be consistency in what they say and do, or their authority is undermined, potentially catastrophically. We keep seeing examples across many sectors and in policy-making circles too, where gaps between talk and action precipitate the downfall of those at the top.

This is a profound shift. Centuries-old, patriarchal power structures are being very rapidly replaced by more diffuse, shared and democratic influence. Different skills are needed to lead now, skills that, as we shall see, tend to favour women's ways of working and behaving.

Not everyone recognises this yet. While there is an emerging realisation that being 'in charge' is not what it used to be, there is still only a vague appreciation of the wide-ranging ramifications. Much carries on as before, in big ways and small: I am frequently asked by executive search firms for my recommendations for 'diverse' board directors and am repeatedly disappointed by the 'old school' lists they show me. There is still a game of musical chairs at the top – and this is a mistake. In the US, around 80% of the fifty largest public companies are connected to each other through one or more shared board members; in the UK, the tendency is to 'recycle' FTSE-100 chairmen, making that prized role still very much a male bastion.

The wheels of change may be turning very slowly at the top but the broader power shift is not a short-lived surge in populism. Unless we put the technological genie back in the bottle, it is irreversible and means leaders, companies and policy-makers need quite different ways of thinking and skill sets to be relevant, successful and genuinely powerful. We talk blithely of 'disruption' in business – when revenue streams built over decades can be grabbed by start-ups over a matter of months, if not weeks – but few seem to have grasped that this extends to power structures too.

The far-reaching impacts of this power shift can be compared with the wide-ranging (and often breathtakingly fast) impact of the internet on many traditional businesses. The retail sector is an obvious example. Even the most traditional, 'heritage' retailers are forced to address the vast challenge of online shopping opportunities. A few firms have been the disrupters, others have embraced the change, a third group is plodding along, trying to catch up with shifts that have already happened. In the UK, a number of long-established high street brands have gone into receivership; others struggle to redefine their business. A walk down any British high street – now usually a string of coffee shops, restaurants, hairdressers, nail bars and dentists, alongside a few specialist stores – shows how dramatically our shopping habits have changed even over the past few years.

In 2006, nine retailers dominated the US market; Amazon accounted for just 4% of the group's total market value. By 2016, Amazon was 55% of the total. With over 750 million mobile users – more than four times all of its competitors combined – it has, in the words of John Koetsier, 'won retail', reinventing how we buy and receive products. Amazon achieved this amazing feat by creating a personal (yet automated) connection with their customers, tracking their history and searches to understand their needs – and delivering great service. For retailers – and so many other sectors now – a digital strategy is not peripheral to the main event: it is *the* main event. Companies are *all* technology businesses now.

The irony is that to formulate (and continuously evolve) the right digital strategy, businesses need the right human minds – and that means the right *combination* of minds. It's not a question of digital *or* human, but digital *plus* human.

Companies therefore need to take the optimisation of their talent seriously. The impact of getting it right or wrong may not be immediate, but any company that drags its feet in developing its collective human intelligence will be less likely to succeed than smarter competitors and increasingly disconnected from its customers. Astute companies are already working hard to develop the right *ecosystems*, where their diverse talent helps create an intelligent working environment and strong customer engagement.

Out of this arise exciting opportunities for equality, but we could too easily squander them by failing to see that today's destabilising changes offer the moment for a leap forward in the quest for gender and other equalities. A continuation of the past would not have got us to where we want to be – even if, superficially, it might seem more benign. Whatever you think of Brexit and President

Trump, these votes show that there is an urgent desire for new ways of thinking and new leadership. I think it has been a huge mistake for the establishment on both sides of the Atlantic to dig in their heels, to be dismissive of those who voted for Trump or for Britain to leave the EU, or to try to undermine other 'protests' (in Spain and Catalonia, Italy, Hungary, Poland … the list will continue to grow). Instead, we should be devoting all our energies to creating a constructive way forward. To those who say that's a naïve hope, I challenge back: by talking and *listening to each other*, we soon see points of human connection, similar hopes and fears alongside our differences of opinion. The common ground includes a desire for security; fulfilling work that can enable us to prosper; friendship and love; a sense of belonging; a good future for our children. With strongly empathetic, inclusive leadership, we could move forward together.

My experience in helping to solve a much narrower, simpler problem, the under-representation of women on UK corporate boards, showed me (just as the chance to be Newton's CEO had done) how dislocations can create rare moments of opportunity to seize. Today, if we tap into our own, feminine brand of power, women can contribute much-needed new thinking to solve our problems – and become more powerful in the process. I was definitely on the outside of the real power base when it came to making changes in the boardroom, but was able to become effective by being empathetic and constructive in my approach. I reached out, rather than fought. Girl power, if you like, but not as we may have thought of it before. This is not about adopting the trappings of male power, but about redefining power, *changing rather than mimicking* the power structures that we have been largely excluded from in the past. Many decades ago, Simone de Beauvoir argued, 'The point is not for women simply to take the power out of men's hands, since that wouldn't change anything about the world. It's a question precisely of destroying that notion of power.'

It's been a long wait, but this is our moment to show the strength of feminine power.

Chapter 3

The 30% Club: the strength of feminine power

When you start to develop your powers of empathy and imagination, the whole world opens up to you.

SUSAN SARANDON

Having been appointed in rather unorthodox and dramatic fashion to be Newton's chief executive, I focused on delivering the results that were proof that I was up to the job. Achieving strong results – both investment and financial performance – requires the right team, and with Newton's motto that 'No one has a monopoly on great ideas', my colleagues and I made a deliberate effort to develop diversity of thought and perspective. Just as on a football pitch, the best investment teams are not necessarily groups of the most highly qualified individuals; the interaction between team members plays a vital role.

In common with the rest of the fund management industry, although Newton had a strong meritocracy there were relatively few senior women. I wanted to do something to specifically address this. Young women – both at Newton and in other firms – were often approaching me to ask my advice, usually about combining career and family life, and I was happy to talk one-to-one. It seemed an obvious next step to try to help on a bigger scale. With the encouragement of my Boston-based boss, Ron O'Hanley, I launched a women's initiative for our parent company's European businesses in 2005.

This initiative – like most other companies' gender diversity efforts at the time – centred on networking events, often a talk from a high profile woman. The feedback was always 'how inspiring' but in fact no one seemed inspired to actually *do* anything differently. Over the next few years, we saw little change in the representation of women at senior levels – and no real evidence that this was likely to change any time soon.

Discouraged, I was about to give up when I was invited to give one of those talks myself at Goldman Sachs, as part of their 2009 Diversity Week. Afterwards Goldman hosted a discussion for 15 men and women from different organisations, and everyone shared what they were doing to encourage their female talent. As I listened, I discovered that I was far from alone: everyone was struggling, no matter how hard and how long they had been trying. So much effort, yet so little to show for it. It seemed pretty clear that we must all be doing something wrong.

One of the attendees was Baroness Mary Goudie, a Labour peer. We agreed that we wanted to 'do something' to break the deadlock. The approach needed a complete rethink.

Of course, it's usually much easier to identify a problem than to come up with the solution. There was no reason to believe that the objective of having many more women in senior roles was simply unattainable: there were plenty of ambitious women, plenty of companies keen to see them progress. As I searched for a way forward, I read widely to see whether any companies or countries had managed to achieve better results. I also researched organisational behaviour more generally, and the theories about differences in the ways men and women typically work. The more I thought about it, the more obvious it seemed that most of us were rushing to try to motivate people from under-represented groups without really understanding what was on their minds, or how our diversity efforts would fit in with the rest of their experiences at work.

I came across a number of interesting practical ideas. One was an effort by Deutsche Telekom to ensure that there were at least 30% women at all levels of seniority. I liked that specific, numeric target and realised that most of us were making a mistake in not setting clear goals. We needed to measure our progress (or lack of it) and have a way of tracking women's advancement just like our other business objectives. The literature I was reading on group behaviour suggested that 30% was a point at which critical mass was reached – and that resonated with me personally. As I thought about my own experiences, being the only woman in the room made me feel self-conscious and I chose my interventions carefully on those occasions. If there were several items on the agenda where I might have a different opinion from the rest of the group, I would speak up about just one or two. If there were three women out of ten people, I was just another person in the room and felt confident to speak freely.

The way in which Deutsche Telekom was promoting its ambition was also appealing: 'Taking on more women in management positions is not about the enforcement of misconstrued egalitarianism,' said the company's then chief executive, René Obermann. 'Having a greater number of women at the top will quite simply enable us to operate better.' Not only was the statement striking in deliberately distancing the move from political correctness and towards the business case, but it was all the more impactful coming from a man.

I realised that women talking to women about women's issues was never going to get us very far. We can encourage each other and feel less alone, but we are likely to need those in leadership positions – mostly men – to help us actually succeed, to open those doors that may be half-closed. This is nothing to be embarrassed about: men on the way up in their careers have long had champions or sponsors in more senior positions, who act as a sounding board, give them a reference, or even line them up for the next role.

But it still wasn't obvious how to pull these thoughts into an action plan, so Mary and I invited almost all the senior businesswomen we knew to a lunch to solicit their input. Over forty came along. I stood up and suggested we needed a new approach if we were to break the deadlock and see more women fulfil their potential in our businesses. Some of those present made it clear afterwards that they did not want to be part of a specific women's initiative, expressing concerns about how that would be perceived by their male peers. Later, I'm happy to say, and particularly after men had joined the campaign, a number of those women became generous supporters. Others were sceptical about the idea that we might ever be able to find a better way forward, after so many years of disappointing progress. All they could see ahead was an extrapolation of the past.

But a new opportunity was arising just as we were having these discussions. As is so often the case, what we actually needed was a vision, not a spreadsheet. The cataclysmic global financial crisis had thrown up a new possibility for us to explore. As analysts, regulators and policy-makers pored over the wreckage of the financial collapse, it seemed obvious with hindsight that bank boards and management teams comprised almost entirely of conventional, middle-aged, affluent men were inherently flawed. The directors might be individually brilliant, but if they were cut from the same cloth, educated similarly and moved in the same social circles, they were far more likely to back each other's opinions than to challenge them.

'Groupthink' is far from a new concept: the term was devised in 1952 by American William Whyte, who used it to refer to similar people not just agreeing with each other but more perniciously believing that they are 'right and good' as well, and so excluding dissenting voices. It's not an unusual phenomenon; many catastrophes long before the 2008 financial crisis have been blamed at least in part on groupthink, including the January 1986 space shuttle *Challenger* disaster, when the shuttle broke up within two minutes of take-off, killing the seven crew members. The analysis of what went wrong showed how the inconvenient truth spoken by engineers concerned about the risks of launching in unusually cold conditions was disregarded by NASA managers in their 'go fever'. A decade earlier, psychologist Irving Janis had studied American foreign policy disasters and identified eight symptoms of groupthink. The symptoms include the illusion of invulnerability, minds closed to warnings, the stereotyping of dissenters as stupid or biased, and pressure on group members to conform or be silent.

Sadly, it seems hard to learn from our mistakes. The subject matter was different in the financial crisis but the hallmarks of groupthink were present again. By early 2010, the realisation was growing that the boardroom, described by former fund manager Lord Myners in 2008 as 'a retirement home for the great and the good', needed a big shake-up. The door was ajar for different 'types' of people to become directors and an obvious place to start was to address the scarcity of women on boards.

In 2008, fewer than 12% of the directors at the UK's top 100 listed companies were women. Almost a quarter of those companies had all-male boards. Royal Bank of Scotland had just one female director out of eighteen at the time of its ill-fated acquisition of ABN AMRO that precipitated the bank's downfall. Many of these board members had very similar backgrounds, too – in fact, studying a picture of the 17 male directors at the time is like playing a game of 'spot the difference'. It may be hard to believe, but the boards of the next 250 biggest UK listed companies, the FTSE 250, were even more male-dominated. In 2008 less than half of FTSE-250 companies had any female directors at all and the average representation was just 7%. Besides risking groupthink, 93% men is clearly not representative of society or (almost) any company's customer base.

This was a big, emerging and brand-new opportunity, so I persevered with the idea of doing something different, despite the lukewarm feedback. I arranged a smaller lunch for 14 women out of the group of 40 who had responded positively. We were meeting on a Monday; the Friday before, I suddenly felt anxious that we might have yet another inconclusive conversation. I emailed attendees, suggesting the specific idea of the 30% Club. Over Monday's lunch we agreed on a simple, narrow but ambitious goal: to reach 30% women on UK company boards over the following five years through voluntary, business-led change. The members of the Club needed to be the chairmen of the boards, since these were *their* boards and they had the authority to change things.

Of course, they were almost exclusively chair*men* – at the time, just a single FTSE-100 company, Land Securities, had a female chair, Dame Alison Carnwath. Dame Alison has been a fantastic supporter of the 30% Club – but we needed more than one. So that very same afternoon, we tested out the 30% Club idea on two highly regarded and prominent FTSE-100 chairmen: Sir Roger Carr, then chairman of Centrica, and Sir Win Bischoff, then chairman of Lloyds Bank. Would they support a campaign led by chairmen aimed at reaching 30% women on boards? Both immediately said yes. In their own words, 'when we have women on our boards, the dynamic is better, the decision-making is better – but there are too few of them'.

Sir Roger's and Sir Win's evangelism transformed the thinking around the issue. There were many dissenters and sceptics to start with, but the endorsement of these leading, male captains of industry made others sit up and take note. Maybe, just maybe, the under-representation of women on boards was about more than 'just' fairness? A new dynamic began to develop, encouraging more business leaders to join in. This different angle also proved newsworthy: when we launched later that year, with seven founding chairmen supporters, the *Financial Times* ran both a cover story and a prominent interview featuring Sir Roger and Sir Win. The message was clear: the scarcity of women at the top was no longer a women's issue but *everyone's* issue. Men and women were going to work together to resolve it.

But evangelism does not necessarily lead to results. Another newspaper wrote at the time that the 30% Club had a worthy ambition but 'was very vague about how it was going to achieve it'. I soon realised that this vagueness was in fact an essential ingredient. Nothing had worked before so we needed to draw up a new map to reach our destination. We were wholly open to fresh ideas; we listened and adapted quickly as we made progress or encountered setbacks. Most of the time it was like driving in fog: we could see the immediate few feet in front, but the rest of the route was unclear. As long as we kept progressing, and learning from what was working and what wasn't, we could reach the goal. I became a great believer in pilots to test ideas quickly rather than endless theorising. After all, we knew we *had* to experiment to make progress.

The approach the 30% Club took was to *think big, start small but start now.*

The fear of what might go wrong

In 2016, Harvard Business School Professor Iris Bohnet, the author of the acclaimed book *What Works: Gender Equality by Design*, wrote a case study about the rapid rise in the number of women on UK boards, something that has so far eluded the United States. Iris invited me over to help teach the case study to the first group of students. I had never even been to a Harvard MBA class, let alone taught one, and it was a fascinating experience. Professor Bohnet split the 80 students into five groups, each role-playing one of the parties involved (the government, the cross-party task force established under Labour peer Lord Mervyn Davies, the 30% Club, the executive search community and investors). The students' first task was to list the difficulties they saw ahead. I then explained what had actually happened, whether the anticipated problems arose and how we overcame them. It was an intriguing exercise. The students came up with a cumulative total of no less than 53 potential problems. Many did arise and I started my remarks by noting that it was lucky I had not heard them before we embarked on the campaign, as it would have seemed an impossible task.

It is so easy to come up with reasons *not* to do something. There is always something that might go wrong. It is often very hard to envisage how to navigate through problems before they arise – but when we encounter them, I've found, we can often cope and find a way through. It's very important not to panic at the lack of visibility or the unexpected twists and turns but to see that as part of the journey. That holds true in our careers as well as our personal lives, and helps us achieve so much more than if we hesitate over each step for fear of not being able to see the next or of how we will cope when we get there.

As it turned out, despite the wobbles and setbacks, the 30% Club's timing caught the mood of the moment. The financial crisis created real appetite for change, then a few months after the 30% Club launch, Lord Davies concluded his cross-party public review into the scarcity of women on UK company boards. He made ten recommendations: like the 30% Club, he backed voluntary action rather than mandatory quotas. Lord Davies told me at the time that he had a number of reasons *not* to recommend legislation: one was that his daughter would 'never speak to him again', another was that the 30% Club chairmen supporters had promised that if given the chance, they would deliver progress through voluntary action.

Over the next five years the Davies Steering Committee and the 30% Club formed a powerful double act, combining supportive public policy with private sector action. By the time we reached our shared self-imposed deadline of end-2015, the results for the FTSE 100 fell between Lord Davies' 25% and our 30% goals. Over 26% of FTSE-100 board positions were held by women (we finally broke past 30% in September 2018) and there were no longer any all-male FTSE-100 boards. The next biggest 250 companies had achieved even more progress from their weaker starting position: nearly 20% female directors (over 27% today) and just 15 all-male boards (now down to five).

This wasn't an extrapolation of the past, it was a big leap forward.

It was very exciting to see this jump in the numbers – but even more exciting to see a change in the *thinking*. The

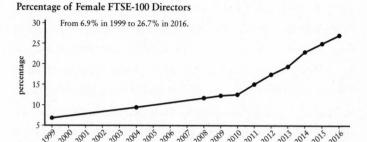

Percentage of Female FTSE-100 Directors

From 6.9% in 1999 to 26.7% in 2016.

issue was now being seen through a different lens. And success led to more success, increasing the acceptability of what we were aiming for so that eventually it just became *expected*.

In November 2011, I interviewed Sir Philip Hampton for the 30% Club website. At the time of our interview he was chairman of the Royal Bank of Scotland, having taken that role after the bank had been bailed out. One of his immediate tasks was to appoint a new board. It is unusual for the chairman of a big company to have carte blanche and Sir Philip talked me through his thought-process. The previous 18-member board was far too big, as well as homogeneous. Sir Philip set about creating a 12-member board, with at least three women, some international experience relevant to RBS, and also, as he put it to me, a blend of experienced directors with fresher faces. He wanted diversity of character and background: 12 former CEOs would not make for a good boardroom dynamic.

As we were talking, he said he wanted to tell me something that he thought I would find encouraging. Every year, a group of FTSE-100 chairmen gathered for lunch. They had met almost exactly a year before, when the 30% Club had just formally launched. The conversation turned to the initiative, and there was a very brief discussion about whether this was something that should be supported – Sir Philip said that it was quickly closed down as 'not really for us'. The same annual lunch had taken place just the week before Sir Philip and I were meeting. This time, the topic had been extensively discussed and there was no question over whether to support the initiative. Instead, the chairmen were asking each other what they were doing to actually meet the target. What a difference a year can make.

But it wasn't just the zeitgeist or the combination of voices that made an impact. The 30% Club's tactics were different from anything that had been tried before – in some respects deliberately so, in others more a stroke of luck.

Through both the campaign's successes and failures, I learned a lot about how to effect change. I believe it's a replicable formula that can help us reach our bigger ambition of gender equality.

There were seven success factors. I've mentioned five:

- seizing the opportunity created by dislocation
- focusing on the business aspects, rather than 'merely' the fairness issue
- having a measurable goal with a deadline to create urgency

- involving men with the ability to change things, and
- being open to new ideas.

The sixth was something of a 'fake it till we make it' approach. The 30% Club took one step forward but we would act as if we had taken two. We talked up the progress, we celebrated good stories, we were confident. This did not always come easily. But I could see that people wanted to become part of a successful movement and that there was a circularity to that success. The more progress we made, the more progress we were likely to continue making.

The intriguing aspect was, the bolder I became in my requests, the more likely the response was to be 'yes'. One particularly ambitious event was a Washington DC breakfast, generously hosted by KPMG, and deliberately planned to coincide with the 2014 IMF conference. The US chapter of the 30% Club had just been launched and while Peter Grauer, the dedicated and energetic founding chairman supporter, would be on the West Coast at the time talking to Silicon Valley entrepreneurs about the campaign, we saw an opportunity to raise the 30% Club's global profile just before the IMF's official business got under way in DC. Mark Carney, Governor of the Bank of England and father of four girls, would be attending the conference so I asked Sir Roger (who was then serving as a non-executive director on the Bank's Court – this is a tight-knit community) if he could see whether the Governor might be prepared to speak at our breakfast.

The answer was encouraging but not definite. The Governor's office explained they could not 'mark-up' his diary but said that Mr Carney was minded to accept if he was free. This left me in something of a bind. I wanted to encourage global bank chiefs to come to the breakfast, but they were much more likely to do so if the Governor was speaking. I spent a week of our family summer holiday hand-writing notes (which kept flying into the hotel pool) to invite CEOs and policy-makers to the event, indicating that we *expected* the Governor to be our speaker. Meanwhile I kept the Governor's office up to date with the list of *expected* influential attendees, as that would surely increase the chances of his attendance. Brenda Trenowden of ANZ Bank, who later took on the mantle of leading the 30% Club, worked tirelessly to round up those accept-ances. Finally, it was confirmed that the Governor would speak. Unlikely as it seems, this whole precarious plan, infused with a dose of bravado, paid off. The room was full of influential men and women and the Governor spoke openly and eloquently about the Bank's 300-year tradi-tions and the importance of diversity in creating a modern culture. The bank CEOs, seated at tables at the front, took turns with the microphone to contribute their own thoughts and ideas about how to accelerate progress around the globe. Nothing ventured, nothing gained.

The 30% Club's final key success factor was taking a *feminine* approach to solving a business problem.

The word 'feminine' divides people. Some object to the very idea that there are characteristics more generally associated with girls and women. Of course, there can be as much (or more) difference between individuals of the same gender as between the genders. That is, in my view, perfectly compatible with using the words 'feminine' or 'masculine' to describe traits more *commonly* found in either girls or boys. It certainly doesn't mean that those words apply to every *individual* girl or boy.

I've also encountered the anxiety that by using the term we may perpetuate gender inequalities. In fact, I believe the opposite may be true. If we understand each other's (*average*) differences better, we can develop more 'gender intelligent' strategies to encourage both men and women to thrive, rather than try to force everyone into a system that tends to motivate one or the other. It's important to recognise that we can be *equal but different* if we're really going to achieve progress.

"Do you think the directors ever pretend to be us?"

Punch Magazine, August 1971

It's a contentious topic, and we'll explore it more fully in the next chapter. For now, let's use 'feminine' as perhaps imperfect shorthand for the approach that defined the 30% Club. We were not looking to assume the traits of the group that we were aiming to join – not trying to simply replace a few men with a few women who were just the same. The goal was, and remains, more diversity of thought, of approach, of behaviours. The 30% Club's approach therefore *emphasised*, not downplayed, difference and in particular the qualities associated with women and girls: empathy, social sensitivity, collaboration, kindness and gentleness.

Encouraging voluntary action rather than legislation or quotas to achieve our goal of more women on boards was the most obvious manifestation of this feminine approach. Forcing people to do something would have completely undermined what we were trying to do. Quotas are very much command-and-control, a confrontational rather than an empathetic approach. Few people seemed to understand this, focusing on the speed of attaining results, not what those results really signified. The 30% Club's ambitious goal was that men and women would become unified in *desiring* boards with a better gender balance, and that this would help improve culture throughout their organisations, as well as increasing the numbers of women on boards. We wanted to ensure not only that the very best people serve on boards, but to open up the definition of 'best' so it did not mean 'just like the existing directors'.

Another symptom of our feminine approach was to be open source, to partner not only with the Davies

Committee but with many others who were already doing great work in this area. There was no sense of competition, helped by the fact that the 30% Club was not a diversity business, simply a group of business leaders focused on achieving results. Members of the Steering Committee included leaders of successful initiatives like the Professional Boards Forum, which introduces chairmen to women with the 'undiscovered' potential to be non-executive directors. The Forum stages events where candidates solve fictitious boardroom problems: its success rate (attendees appointed to boards) is impressive, with more than 50 alumnae appointed as non-executive directors to date. We had no desire to reinvent the wheel but looked to provide cohesion to fragmented efforts, as well as fill in any gaps.

Through this joined-up approach we created a ripple effect, gradually widening out our radius of influence. Importantly, that included the media, which got firmly and consistently behind the campaign, amplifying our voice. Heather McGregor, now Professor McGregor, Dean of Edinburgh Business School, then Mrs Moneypenny, *Financial Times* columnist and one of our brilliant 30% Club Steering Committee members, was instrumental in keeping the story on the front pages. Everyone involved was generous with their time and expertise; numerous intensive research projects were conducted on a 'pro bono' basis, as was the broader publicity campaign, masterminded by Gay Collins, another stalwart member of the Steering Committee. It was incredible really seeing how determination and dedication could achieve so much, with no money changing hands.

Without being especially conscious of it at the start, we were drawing towards us people with the ability and authority to change things, to the point where they believed in the desirability of the goal. If they came to think of it as their own idea, so much the better. I discovered a new power of persuasion in myself, intensified by strong allies. Sir Win Bischoff spoke about my tactics onstage at a dinner some years later in New York: 'Without us realising what Helena was doing, she was getting us to do the work,' he said, with a broad smile. Several of the chairmen and I became good friends; it was fun making progress in such a positive, harmonious way. The chairmen came up with many of the specific ideas: Sir Win made an impromptu announcement onstage at one 30% Club event that we would now set a 30% target for women in executive roles and, in front of the bemused audience, asked me, as I sat in the front row, what timescale we should set for that. Sir Roger suggested that chairmen *deliberately* instruct search firms to look beyond their comfort zones and specifically at least one level below their normal seniority levels for boardroom candidates. Robert Swannell, then chairman of Marks and Spencer, kept up the pressure by stating frequently that he would rather have joined a 50% Club.

I soon saw just how much more could be achieved once those on the inside campaigned for those on the outside to join them. I firmly believe that male champions of change are important if we are to see real progress. For a start, men saying they wanted more women to join them were so much more convincing than if I'd said we should have the opportunity. Stated by a woman, the message can seem self-serving or become blurred with the fairness argument; stated by a man, the business case is – for now – heard more clearly.

The idea that men in positions of influence can be highly effective champions of gender equality is nothing new. In 1848, Frederick Douglass, a leader of the American anti-slavery movement, strongly defended Elizabeth Cady Stanton against criticism of her 'Declaration of Sentiments', a statement of women's rights modelled on the United States Declaration of Independence. In Britain, John Stuart Mill, the eminent economist, philosopher and also then a Member of Parliament, presented a petition in 1866 to the House of Commons in favour of women's suffrage. The following year, he added an amendment to the 1867 Reform Act, which was aimed at giving many more working men the vote: Mill substituted the word 'person' for 'man'. His amendment was defeated by 194 votes to 73 but helped the suffrage movement to gain momentum and Mill continued to advocate strongly for equal rights for women. He wasn't exactly typical, however: fifty years later British suffragette Emmeline Pankhurst called on men to champion the cause of women's right to vote in her famous 'Freedom or Death' speech, recounting, 'One woman broke the windows of the Guard Club ... some of the guards came out and they said "Why did you break our windows? We have done nothing." She said, *"It is because you have done nothing I have broken your windows."'*

In 1926, Serbian-American inventor, engineer and visionary Nikola Tesla gave an interview published under the title 'When Woman is Boss'. Tesla foresaw the dramatic impacts of wireless technology alongside the 'acquisition of new fields of endeavour by women'. He asserted, 'It is not in the shallow physical imitation of men that women will assert first their equality and later their superiority, but in the awakening of the intellect of women.'

And critically, men can be the most powerful advocates not only for women's progression, but also for appropriate behaviours towards us. Ben Bailey Smith, better known by his stage name Doc Brown, is a leading and compelling advocate for men to be respectful to women. Speaking at a school in 2013 he pointed out to his male audience, 'Men that are older than us have somehow created a world where we're supposed to believe that girls are somehow secondary to us.' He added, 'we have the power to change that, you have the power, I have spoken because now people listen to me'. I met Ben when we were both being interviewed on *Woman's Hour*, and he told me that when he started working to improve attitudes towards women, particularly amongst young black men, he experienced a backlash from some of his fans who challenged him, saying he wasn't 'cool'. Ben has two daughters and a famous sister, the novelist Zadie Smith, and is convinced that weak men prey on the vulnerable, whereas strong men will use their power to improve things, including railing against the objectification of women.

The history of feminism shows how the involvement of men has ebbed and flowed, varying from times when men – often just a few enlightened individuals – have proactively sought to help correct what they have recognised as a wrong – to episodes of 'sisters doing it for themselves'. When I was a child, the 'second wave of feminism' (the suffrage movement being denoted the 'first', although there were earlier advocates of women's rights) was in full swing and the image portrayed by the media was that feminists were anti-men and militant. *A woman could be a feminist or feminine but not both.*

The words actually spoken by women at the time suggest that this was not an accurate picture. On 22 March 1971, the date of my fifth birthday (in case you're wondering, I wasn't actually listening at the time), American academic and feminist activist Kate Millett was interviewed by Sue MacGregor on BBC Radio 4. Millett suggested that 'men and children, as well as women, could live much freer lives without this oppressive, patriarchal social system'. The presenter summed up her ambition: 'You're not out for an equal slice of the cake as it stands today, you're out to change the recipe.'

But there was little receptivity to this way of thinking in the 1970s, and the message became distorted. In the same interview, Millett suggested that many of the ideas of the feminist movement at the time were being misrepresented and portrayed as destructive because the establishment felt 'very threatened'. She stressed that, contrary to reports, the movement was 'not out to demolish anything' but was looking to build new, additional lifestyle choices and for basic human rights to be bestowed on women. The goal was not that women take on the 'oppressive' qualities of the very system they were trying to change: specifically, she said, she hoped for less of the violence associated with masculinity.

This really is possible now. I see men everywhere (although admittedly not *every* man) looking to encourage women and girls, welcoming our progress rather than feeling threatened by it. They are conscious of the changes in our world, aware that the 'old' system needs changing too, and are often extra-motivated by talented daughters. When the 2015 Oxford and Cambridge Women's Boat Race finally – after 186 years – took place on the same day over the same course as the men's race, helped by Newton's sponsorship, I was a little unsure how it would be received, given the iconic status of the (men's) Boat Race. As Newton's then-CEO, it was wonderful to be greeted warmly by many, including men, as I walked with my husband along the pathway by the Thames, and as my whole family watched at the finish line. The overwhelming feedback was that the women's presence 'modernised' the Boat Race and that it was 'about time too'. That reaction revealed just how far we have already come.

It is a sign of confidence and strength now for men to support gender equality; we should extend our hand to them, to work with the men in power today to create a world where that power is shared. We should use our feminine qualities to work collaboratively and achieve far greater progress together, as the 30% Club did on a small but symbolic scale to create change in the very traditional British boardroom.

To become equal, but to stay different.

Chapter 4

Men, women, equal, different

I think the fallacy is to think that Women's Liberation meant that men and women would become interchangeable. That has not happened, and most men and women would not want it to happen.

CHRISTINA HOFF SOMMERS

As the mother of nine, six girls and three boys, I sometimes say – only half jokingly – that the Morrissey family offers a big enough sample size for me to be quite confident that there are clear behavioural differences between the sexes. There is, of course, no linkage between my children's gender and their intelligence, and the nine span a wide spectrum of academic abilities, personalities, creativity and very many other characteristics. But when it comes to emotions and relationships, there are certain aspects of how the girls usually behave that differ from their brothers.

The girls are emotionally attuned, quick to pick up on one family member feeling upset or not quite themselves, and keen to talk about their feelings. Our sons are generally more matter-of-fact; they wouldn't necessarily pick up on someone's downbeat mood or voluntarily discuss their emotions. There are significant variations, of course, and considerable differences between the boys and between the girls (at each end of the spectrum, or on specific occasions, a daughter might behave in a more 'masculine' way than a son), but a gender pattern exists nonetheless.

The boys and girls also tend to have different interests and enthusiasms, again not perfectly delineated but still noticeable biases in their preferences. As small children, both girls and boys tended to play with 'gender-stereotypical' toys – even though the younger members of the family could choose whatever they liked from the rather big selection we had amassed by the time they came along. Richard and I never encouraged the girls to play with dolls or the boys with cars or trains – they just chose them. The girls have taken an interest in decorating their bedrooms and picking out their clothes, even as toddlers. The boys have rarely expressed a view on decor or clothes, except when they really don't like my suggestions.

And their friendships differ, too. The younger girls often ask for playdates, keen to initiate social contact, and when one has an argument with a friend at school, the upset tends to linger. A great deal of thought goes into who to invite to their birthday parties when we can't invite the whole class; they discuss who gets on with whom, not just their own 'best friends'. As children, the boys were happy to go to a playdate or a party if asked or arranged for them, but they could 'take it or leave it'. They would know very clearly who they wanted at their own celebrations, although they haven't really been so interested in having these as their sisters. Team sports have been their main social activity. And if they got into an argument with someone at school, they picked up with them the next day as if nothing had happened.

The boys and girls approach exams in distinct ways, too, perhaps partly as a result of their schooling as well as innate differences. The boys tend to carry on much as usual, playing a great deal of sport right up to even the most important public exams. The girls focus entirely on their studies, ceasing all social activities for many months beforehand, carving the odd half hour out of their revision schedule to eat, but shunning all distractions. As I was writing this, 17-year-old Millie came home from school after a week of mock A levels, complaining that her joints had gone stiff 'because it's been so long since I did any exercise'. Millie is sporty, plays netball well, enjoys tennis and loves activity holidays. Her older brother by just a year, who had the same university offer, went on a 15-day school cricket tour in Sri Lanka ahead of his mocks (along with a number of his peers) and comfortably got his grades and place.

The results seem much the same, the preparation very different. I confess to being just like my daughters, study-ing every hour of the day (my sister reminded me recently that included Christmas Day, which I am not proud about). I was always pushing myself to achieve the next goal but at the time didn't really consider where it might all lead to, or look to gain broader experience. I've come to recognise this as a typical conscientious girl's approach: concentrating on the finishing line that's immediately ahead, on getting the next certificate, badge or grade. The trouble is, developing a great career is not like passing an exam. There is no test date, no objective assessment, no certificate. There are relationships to navigate and risks to be taken, failures that will inevitably be incurred as well. We need to prepare young women for that.

Learning to deal with failure is a particularly difficult – and yet essential – skill for girls. We need to understand that failure is inevitable, that it's not just OK to fail but part of life. Winston Churchill was right to say that 'Success is not final, failure is not fatal: it is the courage to continue that counts.'

In my experience, girls' fear of failing is often stronger than boys'. I'm sorry to say that our older daughters exhibit much more self-doubt than their brothers. Their conversations are peppered with 'I'm not very good at that' or 'I don't think I can do it', and when my husband and I try to help them choose exam subjects or courses, they start by excluding weak areas rather than listing strengths. It is exasperating, but also makes Richard and me feel sad that they do not appreciate their own talents. They can spot the problem in others: aged sixteen, our daughter Clara wrote her application to become a school prefect. She observed that the younger girls in the school were 'greatly hindered by self-doubt and I would like to help others overcome this. So many girls miss out on opportunities because of this fear of failure.' Insightful, accurate comments. Yet when I asked Clara (who is a wonderful, prize-winning artist as well as academically strong) if she felt confident in her own ability to succeed she replied, 'Not really, I am afraid that there will be lots of people who are better than me at whatever I decide to do.' As a parent, it's hard not to respond '*Arghhh!*'

I have seen the problem reinforced rather than countered by girls' schooling. At one parents' evening, a form teacher was trying to encourage another daughter, Florence, to continue academic studies and apply for university. Florence is a talented musician who was quite adamant from a young age that she did not want to go to university. I explained that she had applied to a performing arts school, was enjoying writing music and that this was where she saw her future. The teacher looked aghast: 'But she might fail.' 'But she might succeed,' I replied. I have never heard any of our boys discouraged in this way, particularly when they have an obvious talent.

Emphasising the fear factor has an even bigger adverse impact on girls than it would do on boys. A retired teacher friend shared the experience of tutoring his first girls-only A level retake group. Eight weeks into the programme he was alarmed by their lack of progress. He thought about his teaching method and realised that he might need to reconsider the 'more stick than carrot' approach that worked so well with many groups of boys. He changed tack with the girls, praising them and building their confidence. The positive transformation in the girls' performance was startling.

In the workplace we have a much bigger body of (admittedly mainly anecdotal) evidence about behavioural distinctions between men and women. There is general informal agreement that men and women tend to behave differently in some respects. Again, this isn't being judgmental – it's not that men or women are better, just that there are, on average, perceptible differences. Women are typically conscientious, analytical, work well in teams, express their ambition quite subtly or ambiguously and don't tend to promote themselves or think about their careers as strategically as men. Women also seem to worry more, and are introspective; questioning what we have done, going over the issues again and again – and we often visibly show how hard we find it to take negative feedback.

Many of us will recognise feminine or masculine traits, almost intuitively. The debate between friends and colleagues is usually less about whether the differences exist and more about the cause: are the differences biological or the result of social norms? Would men and women exhibit no behavioural differences at all if we were all exposed to the exact same expectations and situations?

My own experiences – particularly as a mother – lead me to believe that both society and biology play a role in determining gender differences. We would still be somewhat different even if exposed to exactly the same circumstances. It is not a minor point: acknowledging and appreciating our innate or biological differences is, I believe, critical to moving on from so many years of frustrating lack of progress towards gender equality in the workplace. I am not a neuroscientist (or any kind of scientist), but as I have sought to understand why our cumulative efforts have not yet delivered that equality, or anything close, I have found that some of the research is very consistent with my practical experiences, in both family and working life.

Debra W. Soh is a neuroscientist based at York University, Toronto. She is candid about the controversies that accompany her work, suggesting that 'people think you're sexist if you argue that there are biological sex differences' in the brain. She points out that 'Sex differences have nothing to do with gender equality. I understand where people are coming from in that they fear these differences will be used to justify female oppression. But instead of distorting science, we should be challenging why female-typical traits are seen as inferior and undesirable in the first place.'

Professor Simon Baron-Cohen is a neuroscientist at Cambridge University who has spent many years researching the differences between male and female brains. He delayed finishing his book *The Essential Difference* because he felt that 'the topic was just too politically sensitive to complete in the 1990s'. He emphasises that overall intelligence is not *better* in one or other sex but relative strengths in different areas are *different* between the two sexes. His theory is: 'The female brain is predominantly hard-wired for empathy. The male brain is predominantly hard-wired for understanding and building systems.'

To many of us, this will seem reasonable, based purely on our personal observations. Of course, we can all think of women who are not empathetic at all, men who are strongly empathetic and women who are highly systematic. The idea though is that, *on average*, women and men exhibit the 'predominant' traits.

Professor Baron-Cohen's hypothesis is based on analysis involving experiments conducted over twenty years. My favourite is one that involved observing over a hundred one-day-old babies whose gender was not disclosed to the researchers. Each baby was shown two 'objects': a human face and a mechanical mobile, coloured and sized similarly to the face. Boy babies showed a stronger interest in the mechanical object, girls showed a stronger interest in the face, based on how long they looked at each. A sex difference in social interest apparent on the first day of life – clearly before any exposure to gender stereotyping.

Professor Baron-Cohen expands on the qualities of empathy and systematising. He describes empathising as naturally tuning into another person's thoughts and feelings – not just reacting to their emotions but reading the emotional 'atmosphere', or being 'emotionally intelligent'. He shows the reader photographs of people's eyes, and invites us to choose which word best describes what the person in the picture is thinking or feeling. On average, women perform better on this 'Reading the Mind in the Eyes' test.

The analysis of biological sex differences might make us feel uncomfortable in a number of respects; we may feel it undermines those who identify as a different gender to their 'birth gender' (or are non-binary). In fact, these neuroscientists make it very clear that there is a spectrum of genders, based on biological markers as well as psychological aspects of identity.

We may still feel wary about exploring biology as a source of explanation of any behavioural differences between men and women but it is much harder to achieve progress if certain ideas are 'off limits'. The controversy around Google engineer James Damore's leaked internal memo, 'Google's Ideological Echo Chamber', shows how we have, at the very least, tied ourselves in knots over the issue. Damore's memo was not 'anti-diversity', as it has been described; it was a challenge to the company's *approach* to diversity and inclusion.

In 2014, there was a wave of media criticism about the lack of diversity in Silicon Valley. Since then, Google, along with several other tech giants, has been trying hard to increase the proportion of female technicians (20%), and significant under-representation of Hispanics and blacks in both engineering and leadership roles (between 1 and 3%). In recent years the company has been completely transparent about the problem, stating 'when it comes to diversity at Google, there's more work to be done.' It publishes comprehensive diversity data on its website, across different job categories and by both gender and ethnicity, covering new hires as well as the existing workforce. (The company also has some of the best-named diversity groups anywhere – 'Gayglers' for LGBTQ employees and 'Greyglers' for their older staff.)

But after several years of effort – and considerable expense, estimated at US$265 million – there's been little improvement in the numbers. In his memo, Damore argued that a dogmatic view of the underlying cause – that implicit and explicit biases hold women back in tech and leadership – was clouding the thinking. He suggested that biological sex differences might have something to do with it, that women and men might tend to have somewhat different skills and interests. Damore took care to point out that 'many of these differences are small and there's a significant overlap between men and women so you can't say anything about an individual given these population level distributions.'

Damore was fired for breaching Google's Code of Conduct – and portions of his memo are inflammatory and simplistic. Silicon Valley's perceived 'bro culture' makes it particularly difficult to separate out the various factors influencing the low numbers of women in leadership as well as technology positions. But if we can't even discuss the possibility that men and women might (on average) be somewhat different for fear of causing offence, we have surely gone way off track. Sticking to one narrow view to explain disappointing progress on diversity contradicts what it *means* to be diverse and inclusive.

The Heterodox Academy was established in 2017 to deliberately encourage diversity of thought at universities and so push against the tide of social and intellectual intolerance at many academic institutions. Its members are all professors who have endorsed this statement:

> 'I believe that university life requires that people with diverse viewpoints and perspectives encounter each other in an environment where they feel free to speak up and challenge each other. I am concerned that many academic fields and universities currently lack sufficient viewpoint diversity – particularly political diversity. I will support viewpoint diversity in my academic field, my university, my department and my classroom.'

Following the Google controversy, the Heterodox Academy's Research Director, Sean Stevens, pulled together a wide range of academic analyses of gender differences, noting 'the presence on both sides of the debate of some of the top researchers'. It is frustrating that so little of the excellent research has ever been widely discussed. The media frenzy surrounding the Damore memo reprised a similar heated discussion in 2005 after then-Harvard President Lawrence Summers suggested that women's under-representation in top universities' STEM faculties might have something to do with 'innate' gender differences. (It's worth noting that Summers' eventual successor, Drew Gilpin Faust, was the first woman to have held that office, following 27 men.) The controversy over Summers' remarks prompted a group of top psychologists to try to settle the argument at the time. The group was impressive not just for its members' impeccable academic credentials; they also represented a wide range of views. At one end of the spectrum, Diane Halpern, former president of the American Psychological Association and author of 'Sex Differences in Cognitive Abilities', at the other, Janet Shibley Hyde, whose papers suggest small and shrinking gender differences.

Sean Stevens summarised the group's 41-page monograph: 'The authors find, over and over again, that the sex differences we observe often have a biological basis yet are not direct readouts of biological processes; they emerge in the course of development and interaction with social processes, norms and stereotypes in ways that can vary across cultures and decades.' This seems a highly plausible assessment; the unanswered questions are why did this compelling review not gain greater traction over a decade ago, and why do so many people still find the subject so controversial?

Diversity is obviously not about being identical – it's about being different, and inclusion is about welcoming those differences, not submerging them. Many diversity efforts are unsuccessful because they are based on pushing women – and other under-represented groups – into the same framework as men. The idea that women need to be the same as men to be as good as men is surely the one we should discourage. Being good at empathising (or history or writing) is just as valuable a skill as systematising (or physics or maths). And although there may be a higher prevalence of certain skills amongst either girls or boys, it should be obvious that even those neuroscientists and psychologists who support the theory of cognitive sex differences do not claim that any skill 'belongs' to either gender. I personally have always been much better at maths than, say, art, and that has made me more suited to a job in finance than fashion, but that doesn't make me better or worse than a designer, just different. The goal is to reach the point where we don't have to fit a narrow mould in order to be valued; a situation where many skills – and the synergies between them – are appreciated.

What resonates with me is the idea that to understand our own behaviour we also have to understand both cultural factors and biology, including how our different hormones affect the ways men and women respond to either successful or stressful situations. After the financial crisis, it was suggested that 'Lehman Sisters' might not have suffered the same fate as 'Lehman Brothers'. One trader-turned-neuroscientist had already researched the idea.

John Coates was a financial markets trader in the 1990s, when he saw how easy it was to get caught up in the dotcom bubble: 'I would see people get on a winning streak on the trading floor and go lunatic. It happened to me as well. For weeks, even months, you feel like the hero of the floor. Every trader who has made money knows what this feels like. You think you're infallible.'

Coates observed that financial market analysts tend to assume that all behaviour is rational. From his experiences on the trading floor, he felt this was a mistake. To form a more accurate picture of financial risk-taking, he decided to research the way our bodies react to winning and losing. Coates studied a group of male traders. He found that on days when traders made an above-average profit, their testosterone levels went up. When their testosterone levels rose, the traders tended to increase their risk-taking. Coates dubbed this feedback loop the 'winner effect'. The problem was that eventually the trader became prone to excessive risk-taking. He would win, take on more risk, win again, and increase the bet and so on … until he risked too much.

Cortisol is the body's 'stress' hormone. It plays a central role in our physiological and behavioural responses to a challenge. Coates' experiments showed that while testosterone rose on days when traders were 'winning', cortisol levels rose more when there was greater uncertainty – higher risk around the returns – rather than simply when the trader was losing. He warned – in 2007, just ahead of the financial crisis – that the acutely elevated levels of testosterone and cortisol he had observed, might 'affect a trader's ability to engage in rational choice'.

Coates suggested that to make the trading floor less vulnerable to irrational behaviour, financial institutions needed to hire more women. Women produce, on average, about a tenth of the testosterone that men generate and are therefore less prone to the winner effect. While he was trading himself, Coates had noticed that the (few) women traders became less caught up in the dotcom euphoria that affected their male colleagues.

The problem is that women aren't particularly attracted to the trading floor – or to the financial sector in general. In my own sector, investment management, just 9% of UK fund managers are women. In the US, only 184 of 7,000 mutual funds are run by women, according to a study by Aviva Investors. It's a chicken-and-egg problem: the male-dominated, 'traditional' image (and reality) of the industry makes it hard to attract women and other under-represented talent. 'Adding in more women' is not, at present, an option. We'll consider ways to break this cycle in Chapter 6.

Unsurprisingly, everyone wants to know whether I think women make better fund managers than men. In my experience, there is often a subtle difference in approach, consistent with all the neuroscience – and what might be seen as gender stereotyping. Like me and my daughters, most female investors I have come across do a lot of analysis, researching their ideas thoroughly, and consider aspects like the culture of a company. Men tend to be focused on the numbers and quality of the management teams (particularly around the clarity of the CEO's vision and 'leadership'). Intuitively, a balanced, well-directed team seems the ideal: CityWire's 2018 'Alpha Female' report, the third in an annual series, bears this out. Mixed gender fund management teams delivered superior investment returns over a three-year timeframe than either female- or male-only teams. It seems the fund management community may have (finally) woken up to the performance benefits: the overall percentage of mixed teams increased by 25% since the first report in 2016.

I love the title of one particular study of gender differences in investment behaviour (of non-professionals): 'Boys will be Boys: Gender, Overconfidence, and Common Stock Investment'. Two distinguished behavioural economists, Brad Barber and Terrance Odean, analysed over 35,000 American households. They looked at the trading patterns and returns achieved by men and women in their investments over a six-year period. They found that men traded *45% more* than women. This is a very significant difference. There are costs involved in trading, which reduced the men's net returns by over 2.6 percentage points a year compared with trading costs of 1.7 percentage points for the female investors. What explains such a marked difference? Odean and Barber thought it was quite straightforward: men were 'overconfident'.

Confident people are more likely to take action based on their views. Other studies and data suggest that men are more confident than women when it comes to financial matters, so trade more often, but their confidence exceeds their ability to add value. (Of course, an *individual* man may be a brilliant and patient investor.)

All these studies corroborate what seems intuitive: that it would be useful to have better balance in decision-making, that men and women complement each other.

If we can agree that men and women often behave differently in certain respects, then the natural next step is to recognise that we are likely to be motivated in different ways as well. Sending women on assertiveness training courses to try to improve their promotion prospects may prove counterproductive. And the language used in many situations can be unintentionally off-putting to women. A leading business school asked me for help: just one woman had applied to its advanced executive programme that year. A quick glance at the brochure offered an easy explanation: the language used was aggressive, militant, describing how the course would enable participants to 'dominate' and be 'world-beating'. This language wouldn't just discourage women from applying, but a lot of men, too.

Awards to celebrate women's success can perpetuate the idea that women need to fit in with the male definition of power. In 2016, Forbes' list of 'The World's 100 Most Powerful Women' celebrated the 'smartest *and the toughest* female business leaders, entrepreneurs, investors, scientists, philanthropists and CEOs'. The magazine applauded their 'formidable achievements', which it described as 'even more so given how hard it can be to establish inroads into industries and job titles traditionally dominated by men'.

Most of the powerful women I know would wince at being described as 'tough'. We don't want to be 'tough' or 'formidable' – nor do I think it would be particularly helpful to the world, our businesses or our families if we were. Instead, we want to apply our ability to connect with others, to be attuned to their perspective – skills that can be very powerful in their own way. Meanwhile 'power dressing' is a misnomer if it means adapting men's suits rather than dressing in a way that shows the empowerment of women in our own style.

We need a broader definition of power, a new feminine brand of power, rather than just fitting in awkwardly with the masculine concept.

If women can be encouraged to be truly women at work, they can make a big difference to the effectiveness of an organisation. In 2011 two American academics, Anita Woolley and Thomas Malone, undertook a study into the collective intelligence of groups. They were looking to establish whether collective intelligence could be predicted and therefore enhanced, based on the characteristics of the individual members of the group. They found little correlation between a group's collective intelligence and the individual intelligence of its members (measured through IQ tests). This was not unexpected: there is plenty of evidence in the fields of sport and music (and in fund management) that the best performing teams are not necessarily the groups of most talented individuals.

The finding that did surprise them was an almost linear relationship between performance and the proportion of women in a team. Their experiments suggested that if a group includes more women, its collective intelligence rises, hitting a peak when women comprise around two-thirds of the team. Simply put, teams comprising mostly women perform *consistently better*. Professor

Woolley admitted, 'This is not something we expected and the first time we observed it we didn't pay much attention to it, until we replicated the finding in different studies.'

As Woolley and Malone probed further, they found that having more women in a team seems to alter the collective thought processes in 'a number of beneficial ways', with the groups displaying greater collaboration and the men also 'changing their behaviour positively'. Professor Malone suggested, 'Many studies have shown that women tend to score higher on tests of social sensitivity than men do. What is really important [to a group's performance] is to have people who are high in social sensitivity, whether they are men or women.'

Studies into the financial performance of companies with more female directors and senior managers corroborate Woolley and Malone's theory that mixed-gender teams tend to achieve better results. There are a number of these real-world studies, such as those produced by McKinsey, Post and Byron, Credit Suisse and Société Générale, analysing companies' empirical results in individual countries, regions and across the globe. The findings are consistent: companies with a critical mass of women on their boards tend to perform better than those without. Credit Suisse, for example, looked at 3,000 companies around the world and found that those with more than one woman on their board had returned an average extra 3.7% a year over those with none in the decade to 2016.

To be honest, however, I tend not to rely on this argument when making the 'business case' for more women in leadership positions or on company boards. (It's interesting that we still get asked for this, given that there's certainly no business case for having only men in charge.)

One of the problems with relying too heavily on the empirical data is that, inevitably, there is much debate over cause and effect: are the best companies in other respects also better at hiring women and then at creating conditions for them to advance, or do the women actually create the outperformance? There's a third possibility too: that smart women tend to join already-superior companies.

It's impossible to prove (we can't eliminate all the other variables or create a 'control group' when it comes to real-life companies) but in practical terms I am not convinced it really matters – there's probably an element of all three in many situations. I was attracted to join Newton because it had an inclusive culture; I was able to thrive as a result of that culture and, in turn, my (feminine) management style probably did help the firm to perform well when I became the boss. There was something of a virtuous circle.

When it comes to the contribution that women are making to a company, we need to consider the context too, including whether the women are able to 'be themselves', to provide genuine diversity of thought, or whether they are very similar to the men in terms of education, class and perspective.

In a 30% Club email exchange following the publication of research from Wharton questioning whether board gender diversity improves performance, Rachel Short, business psychologist, summarised it well:

The situation is more nuanced than 'more women = better performance'. Gender diversity is not a quick fix without attention to the *external context and internal dynamics* of an organisation. Gender diversity is good news for stakeholders – in terms of corporate governance, strategy formulation and corporate social responsibility. And 30% is not a 'nice to have' but a *must-have critical mass*. One or two token women are unlikely to make a positive difference.

For all these reasons I refer to the studies carefully. But with these caveats, the evidence suggests that the presence of more women at the top of a company – not just on the board but running the business day-to-day – is a *useful positive clue* to its prospects.

Julia Dawson led the Credit Suisse team that undertook its 'Gender 3000' research studies. Although we were both working in London, Julia and I first met (as business people so often do) thousands of miles away from our homes, in Toronto, Canada, as the two keynote speakers at a conference. Around 250 investment professionals attended the event, and were able to contribute through (anonymous) electronic voting. The moderator asked the audience to consider a statement: 'Companies with more women in their management teams deliver better financial performance.' The audience, a mixed group of men and women, was asked whether they concurred: 93% of them 'agreed' or 'strongly agreed' and the remaining 7%

declared themselves to be neutral. There was not one single person, in a blind ballot, who disagreed. The *immediate* follow-up question posed to this group of highly qualified, intelligent investment professionals was whether they took account of the number of women in a management team in their company analysis. Only 25% said they did.

This seems irrational. These are smart people: why pay so little attention to something that they say themselves is helpful to returns?

One possible (although unsatisfactory) explanation is that many women executives are not running business units, but heading up service areas like human resources and communications. Investors tend to deal with 'management' – the chief executive, the chief financial officer and heads of business units – so any theory about the importance of women in leadership roles can easily be forgotten

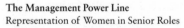

The Management Power Line
Representation of Women in Senior Roles

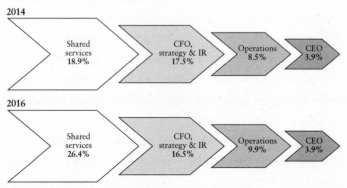

in practice. According to the Credit Suisse 2016 study, only a dismal 3.9% of the CEOs of those 3,000 companies in its data set are women.

We're working hard to encourage more women to progress to CEO level (see Chapter 8). But as companies adjust to the new power models, as the importance of talent development and connections with a wider range of stakeholders (such as their local community) become recognised, women won't necessarily need to move from their current roles to be seen as influential. Reputation, (collective) intelligence and relationships are becoming key to success, *so these jobs will come to be viewed as some of the most important in a firm.*

At present, accounting treatment means that talent is seen as a cost, rather than an asset to a firm – an outmoded concept, but one that is proving hard to change because of the practical difficulties in valuing 'human capital'. I have been involved in a number of projects to try to resolve this. Unilever played host to one seminar: Doug Baillie, then Unilever's Chief Human Resources Officer, explained that his previous role at the company was as President of Western Europe. He was exasperated that financial analysts continued to ask him more about business matters related to his *last* job, although he knew that the company's *future* prospects depended to a large degree on success in his current one.

Even after the loudest wake-up call imaginable in the shape of the financial crisis, I think that many people find it hard to think of diversity as *core* to business success. I've seen how my own efforts have often been regarded as 'extra-curricular' rather than part of what it takes to lead a business today. When I was made a Dame in the Queen's 2017 Birthday Honours list one commentator lamented the lack of 'captains of industry' in the list, described me dismissively as 'mother-of-nine media favourite' and put inverted commas around the citation 'for services to diversity', as if that wasn't really a thing as far as business is concerned.

This perception reflects where we've come from rather than where we're going to. The long history of feminism, racial equality movements, and more recently the LGBTQ+ community's fight against discrimination have been mostly about *fairness* and about respecting each other and our differences. Fairness and mutual respect are vitally important but aren't enough of an incentive to make businesses reinvent themselves. We know that, since otherwise we would have solved things by now. To get results, we need to consciously shift the narrative away from any association with political correctness and towards the language of business. Diversity needs a rebrand.

To date, even the most committed CEOs are typically disappointed with the rate of progress. In practice, the approach has tended to be to add in special initiatives around the edges of long-established existing practices. Mini-makeovers rather than a top-to-toe overhaul and, as such, destined to disappoint. Today's ways of working are largely built around what made sense in the past, before we had technology, for a narrow group of people in a world where roles were clearly defined and when career paths were linear. For a whole host of reasons, not just to encourage diverse talent, we now need to re-devise those working practices, so we can work more efficiently, more intelligently, more productively.

If we stay on same path, making modest and often off-target adaptations, we will continue to be disappointed, and not just by a lack of progress on diversity. Organisations will struggle to keep up with other transformations too – and their diverse talent will fall short of fulfilling their potential. 'Leaning in' is demoralising if what we are leaning in to doesn't suit us – not because we're prima donnas, but just because we don't operate quite like that.

The gender pay gap row in the UK, catalysed by (welcome) new transparency laws requiring companies with over 250 employees to disclose their gender pay gaps, epitomises the problem. The glaring gaps (all in the same direction) between brilliant female presenters and their male peers at the publicly funded BBC have inevitably prompted recriminations. Sir Philip Hampton, who I have witnessed to be a long-standing champion of gender equality, was roundly criticised for suggesting that women 'let it happen'. He said, 'Lots of men have trooped into my office saying they are underpaid, but no woman has ever done that.' My experience as a boss has been similar, but less stark: a few women have requested pay rises but far more men (and usually bigger rises, too). Sir Philip's comments reveal a gender gap in understanding, however.

Women feel less comfortable asking for pay rises and promotions but getting us to behave more like men is surely not the right answer.

Jordan Peterson, clinical psychologist and author of the bestselling book *12 Rules for Life: An Antidote to Chaos*, points out that gender pay gaps are – obviously – attributable to multiple factors. While prejudice does play a part, Peterson suggests that the (average) differences between men and women also have a bearing on the issue. In an infamous interview with Channel 4 presenter Cathy Newman (viewed twelve million times to date) Peterson said, 'There's a personality trait known as agreeableness. Agreeable people are compassionate and polite. Agreeable people get paid less than less agreeable people. Women are more agreeable than men.' Newman says this implies the solution is to make women *less* agreeable and Peterson concurs: 'I often treat people for anxiety, for depression and the next most common category is assertiveness training. I've had many, many women, extraordinarily competent women in my clinical and consulting practices and we've put together strategies for their career development that involved continual pushing, competing for higher wages ...'

Instead of teaching women to be less agreeable (compassion and politeness are surely valuable characteristics), I believe we should be aiming to create organisations where we don't need to lobby to be appropriately rewarded. It should not be a case of 'he who shouts loudest gets the best pay deal'; instead we should ensure that the best talent making the greatest contribution is also the most highly valued. That seems pretty obvious to me! And it's not a forlorn hope: I have had a number of experiences around pay that have shown me how entrenched the system is, and yet how it's possible to positively influence it in a way that is not confrontational. Once, in a scheduled one-to-one over the phone, my boss (somewhat out of the blue) mentioned that one of my male colleagues was 'very focused on money'. It took me a moment to realise that he was preparing me for a disappointing pay review at the end of the year – because my peer had made his own expectations clear and the budget was tight. I knew I needed to speak up, to point out that this was hardly a fair 'system' – but I did find it very uncomfortable. Tentatively, politely, I suggested that pay awards should be based on contributions made over the year, rather than on who was more 'focused on money'. There was a long silence. (The hardest part was not to break this silence: I have a tendency to be garrulous but knew it was important to await his response.) Finally, my boss said, 'You're right. I'm sorry. It should be about the contribution each of you has made.' At the end of the year I felt well-rewarded.

Our approach to gendered pay is a microcosm of the bigger-picture decisions we need to make to overcome today's challenges. We can either keep going as we are, with women learning how to become more confrontational – and so behave less like women. That route risks extending our disappointing progress, exacerbating groupthink and sustaining today's march towards divisive politics. *Or* we can change course, deliberately welcoming difference of viewpoint, style and behaviour, encouraging empathy and humbly trying to learn from our mistakes. That certainly has not happened yet: the financial shocks of 2008 meant that more of those in leadership recognised that diversity of perspective was *desirable*; the 2016 political shocks and their aftermath have shown that the theory hasn't yet translated into practice.

Chapter 5

Diversity of thought: welcome until anyone disagrees!

The reasonable man adapts himself to the world; the unreasonable one persists in trying to adapt the world to himself. Therefore all progress depends on the unreasonable man.

GEORGE BERNARD SHAW

On the morning of 9 November 2016, as the world was digesting the news of Donald Trump's US presidential election victory, a group of business leaders, government officials and journalists gathered in London at KPMG's Canary Wharf offices. The seminar had been arranged several weeks beforehand, not to discuss the US election result (it seemed no one had considered how that might hijack proceedings) but to share the recommendations of a review into the still very low numbers of female executives at UK companies. Sir Philip Hampton, now chair of pharmaceutical giant GlaxoSmithKline, and Dame Helen Alexander, who's sadly since died, chair of events company UBM, were presenting ideas to help businesses improve the gender balance of their leadership teams.

Naturally, the two hundred or so attendees were somewhat distracted by the breaking news of Trump's victory. The atmosphere was strained; it felt odd to be discussing women's advancement on a day when the US election outcome suggested we might be moving backwards. Not only had Hillary Clinton failed to shatter that final glass ceiling in America, but she lost to a man whose campaign had been rocked by leaked tapes of his offensive remarks about women.

The widespread reaction was surprise. Charles Berry, chair of FTSE-250 engineering company Weir Group, was the first to speak on a panel advocating that businesses develop female talent to improve their results. He opened with a telling confession: 'Why was I surprised about Brexit, about Trump? Because the inputs to my thinking were not sufficiently diverse.'

This might have seemed an encouraging admission but it was also disheartening that Charles, a longtime dedicated supporter of efforts to increase boardroom diversity, had not linked that to the need for more diverse 'inputs to [his] thinking'. He was far from alone. Just a month beforehand, I suggested to an American friend, a senior businessman, that Trump would win – only to be told I didn't understand US politics and was wrong.

But why was it all such a shock? Why had the efforts to improve challenge, including but not limited to greater boardroom diversity, not broadened our perspective to seriously consider this possiblity. After all, on the face of it, significant changes had been made. Between 2010 and 2015, 550 new female directors had been appointed to FTSE-350 boards. We had seen good progress in politics, too: in the 2015 UK general election, 191 women Members of the House of Commons took their seats (out of 650). As in the boardroom, progress had been rapid. At this point, a grand total of 450 female MPs had *ever* been elected in Britain, fewer than the number of men (459) sitting in that single Parliament. (We're on a roll – the 2017 general election set a new record, 208 female MPs, 32% of the total.) The motivations behind the drive to attract more female politicians are similar to those in the business world: to represent society better, draw on a wider range of perspectives – and to modernise.

Yet despite these conscious efforts, the fact that the big 2016 political developments on both sides of the Atlantic were such a shock suggested that little had really changed at the top. Conventional wisdom still prevailed – until it was proved wrong. Groupthink remained alive and well.

I have come to appreciate that groupthink is *very* hard to disrupt. In the 1970s, social psychologists Henri Tajfel and John Turner explored the concept of 'social identity', the element of our individual identity and self-esteem that comes from being attached to groups. Rationally, we don't want to self-harm so we don't tend to undermine our group by pointing out where we might be going wrong. So we make collective mistakes, then lock that particular door after the horse has bolted. Bank boards and directors are therefore now subject to much more scrutiny than before the financial crisis, but in fact many underlying organisational practices continue pretty much as before (as the ongoing scandals reveal). In short, we haven't actually disrupted things very much. Some of the faces round the table may have changed but there is still an in-group at the top – and that's true across the world.

It's also true that most of the women who have been joining top company boardrooms are white, affluent, well-educated and middle-aged (yes, like me) just like the men we replaced – a fair and frequent criticism of many of the recent efforts to improve gender equality. There remains much to do to really shake things up, to move beyond a thin veneer of change.

I found this out myself ahead of the EU referendum. I had taken the view – and said it publicly – that Britain would not just survive but be more likely to thrive in the long term if the majority voted to leave. You may be shocked to read that – and that's part of our problem. I really wasn't trying to be provocative. I was genuinely anxious that the financial sector, big business leaders, mainstream politicians and university lecturers might be making yet another groupthink error. Surely the referendum was an opportunity to think carefully about how the world was changing, about Britain's place in that changing world, and the ingredients for future (and more evenly distributed) success? The conventional wisdom was that staying in the EU was the progressive option – but that narrative did not fit my direct experience. I had seen the EU operating in a remote, command-and-control way on issues as wide-ranging as financial market policy and gender-balanced boards (and ironically being especially bullying about the latter, with Justice Commissioner Viviane Reding being completely unwilling to discuss alternatives to legislation). The *opposite* of the approach needed in today's world. In my view, the best decisions are those taken closer to where the real asset, person or community actually is, where there is more likely to be a good understanding of the issues at stake. Distance tends to compound mistakes.

By 2016, we were already seeing the impact of unpopular EU policies on economic and immigration issues; and rising extremism threatening to undermine not just the superstate but so much of what we hold important in our democracies.

After all the focus on the perils of groupthink since the financial crisis, I thought there would at least be room for discussion. We needed thoughtful debate to get closer to the truth. Tellingly, a number of very senior, influential people in the City and broader business said they agreed with me – behind closed doors. In public, however, they were under intense pressure not to say anything at all – one of Irving Janis' classic symptoms of groupthink. The no-platforming of Leave supporters at some prestigious universities was disturbing, stifling genuine intellectual debate and tolerance. A chorus of different voices all saying the same thing is the *opposite* of true diversity. As we approached the referendum, there were plenty of other signs of groupthink: I attended meetings of business leaders where blanket dismissiveness was expressed towards voters for 'not understanding' the economy. There was certainly no attempt to work out why the Remain campaign's scaremongering wasn't resonating or to consider that it might even be the wrong approach (both as a means of persuasion but also perhaps inaccurate as an economic forecast). Instead, the response was to keep on repeating the same message ever more loudly.

The experience showed me rather painfully and personally that we had only reached the point where diversity of thought was welcome in theory, much less so in practice. I could see that my view – and in particular *expressing* that view – made many people, including friends, feel very uncomfortable and even angry. Meanwhile, I found it hard not to feel disappointed that there was no joining up of the dots, that all those diversity efforts we'd been working on together had not actually translated into welcoming or even tolerating difference of opinion. There was no licence to challenge. In fact, it seemed that many of those running businesses or in policy-making roles had become *more* distant rather than better connected since the financial crisis, still operating at the top of their pyramids.

And the problem has only got worse since: the stubbornness seen on both sides of the Atlantic since the Brexit and Trump votes has certainly not helped either country make the best of things. In the UK an obvious, fundamental problem has been the mismatch between those who voted Leave (and won), and those controlling *how* we leave, who (mostly) voted to Remain. Most problematically of all, there has been almost zero attempt to understand the other point of view, and so create a good outcome for *any* of us.

We could learn much from author and businesswoman Margaret Heffernan's compelling TED talk in 2012, 'Dare to Disagree', in which she suggests that in order to think better, we need 'thinking partners who aren't echo chambers' (after the Google episode that expression may sound familiar). Adopting this practice day-to-day certainly can make things less comfortable, much less cosy in the short term, but that's a price worth paying if it means we get closer to the right answer together. Newton's motto, 'No one has a monopoly on great ideas', sounds very inclusive, but also demands an element of disagreement in the decision-making process. When I was CEO, I knew things were working well when debates were heated and the sparks flew. It was time to get concerned when everyone agreed with each other. This may seem counter-intuitive but the more complex our issues and problems become, the more robust and multifaceted our thinking needs to be. The only solution is to introduce more genuine challenge. To deliberately give people the licence to experiment, to come up with new ideas. It's also a 'stitch in time' approach – resolving or even merely understanding our divides early on helps prevent chasms later on.

In her talk, Margaret Heffernan set out the compelling story of Dr Alice Stewart. In 1955, this Oxford medical researcher observed a rapid increase in childhood leukaemia. Her determination to find out the cause was heightened by the tragedy of her own godchild dying of the disease. Most childhood diseases are more prevalent in lower income households, which have less access to good medical care. With leukaemia the opposite was true. Dr Stewart wondered if the cause might lie in the children's prenatal history. So she interviewed the mothers of the children who had died. In what later became known as the Oxford Childhood Cancer Survey, Alice Stewart and her team visited all 203 public health departments around the country to obtain details of every child who had died of leukaemia between 1953 and 1955. As part of the survey, a questionnaire was sent to the mothers of these children as well as to the mothers of children in two control groups – children who had died of other cancers, and children who were alive and well.

Dr Stewart noticed a strong pattern. Children who had died of any form of cancer before the age of ten had been X-rayed twice as often in the womb as healthy children. A single X-ray, well within official safety limits, was enough to double the risk of early cancer. The process already sounds rigorous, but the findings were controversial. *So Dr Stewart charged her statistician George Kneale with coming up with ways to disconfirm the findings.* She deliberately gave him licence to disagree, and when he couldn't disprove the theory, she was confident that it was correct. Alice Stewart published her findings in 1956, to a hostile reception. Nuclear technology was in the ascendancy, and there were many vested interests in its success. The resistance strengthened Alice Stewart's resolve, but it took twenty-five years – and many more tragic childhood deaths – to convince the American and British medical establishments to stop routine X-rays of pregnant women. Vested interests got in the way of intellectual honesty.

For several years, I chaired the Eve Appeal, a small but impressive charity that funds innovative research into gynaecological cancers. These cancers are often detected at a later stage and as a result mortality rates are far worse than for many other cancers. About 40% of the women diagnosed will die of their illness. There has been little improvement in this statistic for many years, with medical breakthroughs proving elusive. The research funded by the Eve Appeal therefore deliberately focuses on 'wild card' ideas. The actual research is just as rigorous as more conventional efforts, involving control groups, years of patient study, panels to review the quality of the methodology. *But the starting point is the licence to experiment, to deliberately challenge conventional wisdom.* Recently, an exciting breakthrough was announced by the medical team working with the Eve Appeal: an 'early warning system' for four women's cancers now, finally, looks within reach. The greatest advances are made when orthodoxies are challenged – in medicine, science, education, philosophy, the arts – and in business too.

I have seen that progress is often resisted, that there will always be those in denial. Many people really don't like change, particularly if they perceive it as undermining a situation that is beneficial to them. I have talked about the enlightened founding chairmen supporters of the 30% Club: in fact, there were just seven at the launch and I received many more protests from those who thought I was interfering, or even, as one chairman told me, 'destroying British business' (amazing, really, what one woman can do). Several years later, Sir Win Bischoff wrote me a lovely and very thoughtful letter, reflecting on the progress we had made together: 'I know from personal observation how difficult, wearisome and often discouraging your efforts and initiatives sometimes were.'

Wearisome though they were, the protests were the death throes of an outmoded view. Within a few years we had seen a paradigm shift in the way the issue of diversity on boards was perceived, so women on boards were now *expected*, as part of a new norm.

In 2017, I received a rather unusual award, from the *Financial Times* in partnership with steel conglomerate ArcelorMittal. They named me 'Person of the Year' at their Boldness in Business awards. An *FT* journalist interviewed me about being bold. She said everyone knew about the triumphs; she wanted to know about things I had done that were bold but had failed. I realised that I couldn't think of any single bold step in business or in life (including having nine children) that hadn't been something of a failure or at least a struggle at certain points. Success and failure are closely intertwined – all the more so when it comes to creating change. Even just challenging what's accepted will disturb some people – and yet if none of us did that, we would never make any progress at all. A degree of courage is therefore needed – as well as support for others pushing the frontiers.

This is where you come in. To take advantage of today's window of opportunity, to deliver on the early promise of more democratic, more equal power, we each have a part to play – CEOs, mid-career managers, the next generation of young women and men as well as their parents and teachers. We cannot achieve our quest by following an established path. This is therefore not the time for received wisdom, dogma or simplistic edicts *either* for women to lean in *or* for businesses to 'fix the system'. It's a time to encourage new ideas, including challenging all those conventional approaches to diversity that have disappointed us, a time to experiment, to see what actually works. We need to create an ecosystem, an interactive, thriving community that does not dismiss, challenge or jealously guard possible solutions but works together, evolving as we learn and so, finally, to get this right.

As the saying goes, it takes a village to raise a child – and to create gender equality.

Chapter 6

Why CEOs need to rethink diversity

If you are a CEO and you don't have gender diversity or diversity in general as a top issue then you've been asleep at the wheel for the last few years.

LORD MERVYN DAVIES

It's hard to find a CEO nowadays who would say that diversity of talent is *not* important to their business. I'd say that most actually believe it, too – the topic is much discussed at leadership levels, and features heavily in lists of companies' 'top strategic priorities'. In contrast with ten or even five years ago, I'm rarely asked *why* it's important but often asked *how* to achieve greater and faster progress.

The problem is, after a decade or more of reasonably intense focus on the topic, the results have been generally disappointing. We've reached a frustrating impasse in many businesses: the management team is discouraged by limited progress, feeling they have already done a lot through numerous initiatives, while scarce diverse talent has become disillusioned. What's more, the 'non-diverse' majority may be (silently) resentful about the time and attention devoted to an issue that they still associate more with political correctness than driving results. Most problematically of all, there's little encouragement of diversity of opinion around *how* to break the deadlock; instead, it's seen as dangerous to question the approach, because that may be interpreted as questioning diversity itself. The result? A persistent adherence to an ineffective set of programmes.

Diversity fatigue may have set in, yet the business reasons for CEOs to master the issue are ever more compelling. Achieving sustained success in the context of multiple transformations is an increasingly complex mission. Simple manual tasks can be accomplished more easily just by having more people do them (in the Morrissey household, many of us clearing the dinner table gets a rather large job done quickly). In complex situations (say, should Clara go to art school or university?), a successful outcome isn't dependent on the number of people involved but on whether we apply the *best thinking* to the problem.

The ascendancy of artificial intelligence has broad ramifications – many as yet unknown – but one that we can see coming fast is a changing role for 'human capital' – people. Elements of current jobs that can be performed by an algorithm will increasingly be done by machines, and those that can't will require judgement, foresight, the ability to interpret beyond mere patterns, and creativity. All roads point to the need for business leaders to devise ways of *thinking better*.

Dr Scott Page is a 'professor of complex systems' and his work focuses on how organisations can improve their thought processes. In *The Difference: How the Power of Diversity Creates Better Groups, Firms, Schools, and Societies*, he proposes that the answer lies in 'messy, creative organisations and environments with individuals from vastly different backgrounds and life experiences'. Dr Page suggests that the link between identity diversity (gender, ethnicity, sexuality, socio-economic background, etc.) and diversity of thought is 'subtle and mysterious' but 'it's clear that an organisation wouldn't want, say, all white men or all Asian women'. He states, 'No one can claim to predict the sources of inspiration, nevertheless, all else being equal, *we should expect someone different – be their differences in training, experiences, or identity – to be more likely to have that unique experience that leads to the breakthrough*' (my emphasis). I love the way he sums up the criticality: 'Diversity should not be a second-order concern – multi-colored sprinkles on the cake of ability – it merits equal billing.'

Julia Hobsbawm is the world's first Professor in Networking, as a visiting professor at London's Cass Business School. In her book *Fully Connected* she suggests that in an unpredictable, less rules-based world, companies that operate more like jazz ensembles than classical orchestras will perform better. Jazz involves spontaneity, improvisation, a degree of letting loose by the individual musician, yet in a band the whole comes together harmoniously rather than being a series of sequential performances. The motif seems apt in our more chaotic, fast-evolving world. A business management team needs to play more like jazz musicians, to be able to adapt, to be inventive rather than depend on a blueprint – and to create a whole greater than the sum of its parts. The leader's role is to optimise – not to organise – that creativity.

CEOs are smart people, attuned to the zeitgeist (OK, some more so than others). They can see that the 'diversity dividend' is only likely to increase. This is especially obvious when it comes to decision-making roles, where the key ideas are generated, where strategy is devised. The value of diversity may be less obvious at the implementation stage, where cohesion around those ideas is important. In reality, many businesses have the exact opposite of what seems optimal: lots of diversity at entry level and much less in the leadership team, even after many years of effort.

The problem is that the majority of diversity programmes put in place several years ago remain stuck in phase one. They haven't kept pace with the evolving thinking. That's not a criticism of the architects of those efforts: any great change is unlikely to be accomplished via the first attempt. It's part of the journey towards progress to stop, assess and adjust, or even start afresh. At this point, what's important is for CEOs to recognise that carrying along the same path will *not* bring their organisation closer to the goal of being truly diverse and inclusive. (It's not a question of ramping things up: redoubling off-target efforts won't make them any more effective.)

One obvious lesson to be learned is that we cannot expect to make progress by simply layering diversity initiatives on top of long-established attitudes and practices. Instead we need a complete overhaul of both working practices and organisational cultures – not only to further diversity but to modernise our businesses to be fit for a disruptive age. We also need to address the anxiety about positive discrimination head-on. Creating an inclusive workplace means just that – it's not about excluding *anyone*. The aim is not to get back to where we started, only with women dominating instead of men.

Correcting the imbalance that has prevailed for decades, if not centuries, requires a really subtle, nuanced approach – but that's pretty much the opposite of the standard initiatives in the 'diversity toolkit' at many companies today. The most frequently used tactic is compulsory unconscious bias training: it's become a big industry in itself, accounting for a large share of the billions of dollars estimated to be spent on diversity each year by American corporations alone. Many technology companies, struggling with especially poor diversity numbers, have embraced it wholeheartedly: Facebook made its Managing Bias course 'harder hitting' in 2015 and 'rolled it out to our teams across the world' when its diversity numbers (around 16% female, 3% Hispanic and 1% black employees) stalled. The company also made the course accessible to others online – with every good intention.

The problem is, there's no evidence that such training works – and good reason to believe it may actually increase animosity towards minority groups. The training itself may convey the idea that managers are part of the problem rather than the path to a solution, while the mandatory aspect causes resentment. Social scientists – and many of the rest of us – have found that people often rebel against rules.

Professors Frank Dobbin and Alexandra Kalev are sociologists at Harvard and Tel Aviv Universities respectively and have studied more than 800 companies to gather the empirical evidence to gauge whether diversity programmes are in fact increasing diversity. The title of their paper, 'Why Diversity Programs Fail', gives the game away. The data they have gathered suggests that command-and-control measures are counterproductive, whereas voluntary measures can be very effective.

Professors Dobbin and Kalev give a blunt summary of their findings: 'your organization will become less diverse, not more, if you require managers to go to diversity training, try to regulate their hiring and promotion decisions and put in a legalistic grievance system'.

Poor Returns on the Usual Diversity Programmes
% change over five years in representation among managers

Type of programme	White		Black		Hispanic		Asian	
	Men	Women	Men	Women	Men	Women	Men	Women
Mandatory diversity training				-9.2			-4.5	-5.4
Job tests		-3.8	-10.2	-9.1	-6.7	-8.8		-9.3
Grievance systems		-2.7	-7.3	-4.8		-4.7	-11.3	-4.1

Diversity Programmes That Get Results
% change over five years in representation among managers

Type of programme	White		Black		Hispanic		Asian	
	Men	Women	Men	Women	Men	Women	Men	Women
Voluntary training			+13.3		+9.1		+9.3	+12.6
Self-managed teams	-2.8	+5.6	+3.4	+3.9				+3.6
Cross-training	-1.4	+3.0	+2.7	+3.0	-3.9		+6.5	+4.1
College recruitment: women	-2.0	+10.2	+7.9	+8.7		+10.0	+18.3	+8.6
College recruitment: minorities**			+7.7	+8.9				
Mentoring				+18.0	+9.1	+23.7	+18.0	+24.0
Diversity task forces	-3.3	+11.6	+8.7	+22.7	+12.0	+16.2	+30.2	+24.2
Diversity managers		+7.5	+17.0	+11.1		+18.2	+10.9	+13.6

(White squares denote no statistical certainty of a programme's effect)

The reality is that we cannot *instruct* people to alter their thought processes and their attitudes. Each of us needs to do that for ourselves. The role business leaders should play is to *encourage* managers and employees to reach their own conclusion that diversity is good news, both personally and for the company. To create a shared goal. That may sound convoluted, difficult to achieve (wishful thinking, even) and perhaps not 'hard hitting' enough, but I have seen that it can be done – and it works. Once the realisation occurs, once people see it for themselves, they start behaving in a more inclusive way and progress can be rapid, real and lasting.

Nobel Prize-winning psychologist Daniel Kahneman and his frequent collaborator, the late Amos Tversky, have been described as 'changing the way we think about thinking'. Kahneman's seminal work, *Thinking, Fast and Slow*, explains that most of our thinking is done 'fast', out of necessity, and – most of the time – our judgements are remarkably sound given how quickly we make them. We use mental shortcuts to function, but that means we are prone to error, bias and fallacies. To make better decisions we need to be aware of this tendency and create workarounds, techniques that protect ourselves and others from inevitable biases.

Harvard Professor Iris Bohnet extrapolates this concept to create 'Gender Equality by Design'. She outlines how businesses can make deliberate process changes to counter biases that stack the odds against women. In the preface to *What Works*, she explains that in 1970, female musicians comprised only 5% of the top five orchestras in the United States. Today, women are 35% of the total players. Progress wasn't achieved through a gradual realisation that women can (obviously) be great musicians; it was catalysed by the introduction of 'blind auditions', first by the Boston Symphony Orchestra, and soon followed by others. When players performed behind a curtain or screen female musicians were 50% more likely to advance to the next round of auditions. That is a dramatic difference. Orchestra directors, in theory only interested in the sound being made, needed a 'workaround' to overcome their gender bias.

Professor Bohnet argues that we should focus our energies on changing environments, not mindsets. In my experience, one can lead to the other. I've seen many times, in many situations (both at work and at home), that changing something 'by design' can ultimately change attitudes too. In my view, it's important that business leaders aim for both, since piecemeal workarounds can't hope to address every eventuality that arises in companies. Our

goal is an evolution that becomes a revolution, where sceptics become enthusiasts and little guidance is – ultimately – needed because the behaviour comes naturally.

You may be dubious, but this is exactly what happened with the 30% Club. The newspaper cartoon on the previous page captured one inherent conflict for potential supporters: by encouraging the appointment of more female non-executives, men could be diminishing their own post-retirement options. Yet even those who might have lost out in this way came to see that it was in their overall best interests to be supportive.

Soon after the launch, I was told that one eminent chairman was disappointed not to have been asked to join, so I started writing to all the FTSE-350 chairs to invite them to become involved. I had quickly learned that handwritten letters are by far the most effective means of eliciting not just a response, but a positive answer. As 350 handwritten letters was too much, I personalised a standard letter, adding notes to tailor the letter to each recipient. This took some time, so I had only made my way down to 'Ha' for Hanson in the alphabet when responses started arriving from the As and Bs. Most were negative, some blatantly hostile, so I put down my pen.

I didn't fight the dissenters (not my style) or tell them they were wrong, even when they had misunderstood what the 30% Club was about, or what I was asking of them. Yet despite this wave of rejection, membership grew from seven founding supporters to over 200. There were two main drivers. The first was a conscious design change in the recruitment process; five of the 30% Club's staunchest supporters (Sir Roger, Sir Win, Robert Swannell, Glen Moreno – then chairman of Pearson, and David Cruickshank – then UK, subsequently global, chairman of Deloitte) became a very high-flying 'recruitment taskforce', persuading their peers to join them (a much more effective approach than my letters). The second impetus came with the recalcitrant chairs starting to see the benefits from being involved, including signalling that they were modern and progressive.

One chairman had been adamant that he did not want to join the 30% Club when I first approached him, and was quite dismissive of the idea. Six months later, he sheepishly – and graciously – said he had made a mistake and was keen to join. I was delighted, but curious to know what had prompted his conversion. He explained that the commercial real estate company he chaired had been on the verge of signing a joint venture when the sole female non-executive director spoke up, tentatively raising concerns. She suggested there were risks around the deal structure that hadn't been considered. The chairman realised she was right, that he and the rest of the board had been too gung-ho in their enthusiasm to get the deal done. The female director had approached the situation differently – *because* of her position outside the group – but nearly didn't say anything because it was intimidating being the only woman. The benefits of the 30% Club were now very clear and the chairman made the *willing choice* to sign up.

I heard Professor Dobbin of 'Why Diversity Programs Fail' speak at a diversity forum in Sacramento jointly hosted by the two vast Californian public sector pension funds CalPERS and CalSTRS. In my own talk earlier at the same conference I observed that the 30% Club chairmen ended up 'wanting what we wanted' and as a result became very committed advocates for change. Professor Dobbin explained what had happened, although at the time I was unaware that the approach was a known technique. He talked about the art of creating 'cognitive dissonance'. That sounds an arcane concept, but is a familiar feeling to all of us – the uncomfortable inner tension when we hold two conflicted thoughts in our mind at the same time. (We feel it acutely if we have to debate the side of a motion we disagree with.) Many chairmen were initially sceptical about the 30% Club but as they started to see the positives, they resolved any inner conflict by changing their original view and getting behind the campaign. I could see the 'penny dropping' in certain conversations – second thoughts that had to come from within a chairman's own mind, that no amount of coercion could have achieved. Several years afterwards, the wonderful woman who masterminded the 2015 Paris Convention on Climate Change, Christiana Figueres, compared notes with me about our respective campaigns. We agreed that the breakthroughs came when people finally realised that progress was in their own best interests – whether or not they actually believed in it.

But the very first step for CEOs – before embarking on the creation of any cognitive dissonance, before even contemplating design changes – is to hold a mirror up to yourself and your organisation. You may have been championing diversity for many years, but consider the following (completely honestly):

1. Do you have a real *strategy* to foster greater diversity of thought – or are the existing efforts a series of tactical measures to improve identity diversity that don't add up to a plan?

2. Do you have the data that forensically shows where the current problems lie? Recruitment? Promotion? Pay? Do you fully understand the processes around each? For example, does the guidance used by your recruiters to filter job applications automatically – accidentally – favour candidates who think in a similar way? When it comes to keeping your talent, are there danger zones around people with certain characteristics or backgrounds – for example, do few women get promoted after maternity leave? Are those from different socio-economic backgrounds than, say, the management team, given opportunities to contribute their own ideas or are they being encouraged to succeed by emulating those at the top?

3. Are you personally listening to the experiences of both diverse and 'traditional' talent? (Large

corporations tend to build many barriers to upward communications to the CEO so you may have to work hard to encourage people to tell you). Do you understand why they feel the way they do? Can you identify the 'kinks in the hosepipe' that prevent diverse talent from progressing? Do you have a mentee – or two? Are those from under-represented groups still outside the 'inner circle'? Have diversity efforts alienated existing traditional talent? Have you made it clear that an inclusive culture means just that, not positive discrimination?

4. Are you encouraging or coercing involvement? If you are already inviting rather than forcing participation in efforts to improve diversity, have you created easy opportunities for staff at all levels to get involved? Have you created an ecosystem where diverse talent can help change things as well as benefit from those changes?

5. Are your initiatives aimed at changing the whole workplace or are they based on the hope that a few more people with diverse identities will be encouraged to fit into existing working practices? Are you prepared to innovate, experiment, even revolutionise? Is it clear that *talent* will rise to the top, although it may not fit a 'classic' mould? Are you (inadvertently, perhaps) favouring certain diversity dimensions over others (e.g. LGBTQ+ over religious diversity), and so undermining

inclusion? Is dissension encouraged, challenge welcomed, and are meetings conducted so that those with ideas feel able to contribute, whatever their level, role or personality?

6. Are your goals ambitious enough? Have you made the explicit link between truly diverse thinking and the future growth of your business (not just in vague, clichéd terms about people being the company's most important asset)? Are some of the smartest people in your business working in Human Resources, reporting directly to you? Are you personally engaged, or have you delegated and so given the impression that this issue is peripheral to 'real' business matters?

7. Is your approach sophisticated? Have you made it clear that you are *not* aiming for a situation where your employees look different but actually think alike? As David Sacks and Peter Thiel put it in *The Diversity Myth*, 'Real diversity requires a diversity of ideas, not simply a bunch of like-minded activists who resemble the bar scene in Star Wars.' Are you clear, both in your own mind and your communications, that you are not looking to merely window-dress, to create the illusion of diversity?

Once you have the answers, don't fight them, work with them. Resist any temptation to tell people where they're wrong or to defend the approach you have taken to date.

If it's clear that the whole topic of diversity has become charged, that it evokes suspicions of political correctness or causes resentment, start by dropping the 'D-word'. Reframe the agenda as a core business objective around thinking better and speak entirely in business terms when referring to the goals around talent (for example, the impact you expect to see on profits). In Chapter 1 we saw how an experiment at Newton, where all staff were offered a four-day working week, made business sense first and foremost. The long-term benefits included better staff retention (saving costs that we might have incurred in replacement hires and possible loss of revenues associated with key staff). It *also* prevented any sense of special treatment for maternity returners wanting a shorter working week. The workplace was better for everyone, not just the women and everyone bought into the programme because it was linked to improving the business.

In all the organisations where I have seen great progress, there's been a winning combination of bold ambition, practical design interventions and skill in motivating people, within a clear – defined, well-communicated – strategy that's core to the business.

Let's look at three areas – by no means an exhaustive list – to get a flavour of how business leaders can create genuine enthusiasm for genuine diversity.

Recruitment

Of course, if a company can't attract sufficient diverse talent at entry level it's almost impossible to make progress in senior roles. I'm often asked whether I believe artificial intelligence is the unbiased recruitment – I'm wary, for reasons we'll return to in a moment. Happily, I have seen instances where great strides have been made in encouraging a much broader range of candidates to apply through more traditional approaches even to companies in sectors like banking.

Over five consecutive summers from 2012 to 2016, I was invited to address financial institution UBS's interns on gender diversity, as part of their training programme. It was a fascinating experience, made all the more so by the progress I witnessed over that time as UBS dramatically broadened the diversity of the intake. Effectively, the group went from predominantly pale, male and private school/Oxbridge-educated to gender-balanced and boasting a rainbow of colours, creeds, socio-economic and educational backgrounds. The first couple of years, the bank asked me to speak to just the female interns; in 2012 that was an audience of around sixty, or 30% of the whole intake, but in 2013 it dropped sharply to just thirty, or 15%. I asked what had happened, and the hiring team explained that there were far fewer female applicants and even smaller numbers made it through the hiring process. I suggested they take a good look at the data for any clues that they could then use for design changes, rather than merely hoping for higher interest from women the following year. We also agreed that it might be helpful for me to speak to the whole cohort in future, as it was important that young men entering the industry were conscious of the issues.

By the time I spoke in 2016, the audience was 50% female, and visibly ethnically and religiously diverse (for example, Sikhs wearing turbans). A woman translated my talk into sign language as one of the interns was profoundly deaf. White, traditionally educated men were still very much present – and now very highly engaged, asking thoughtful questions – and one invited me (and I accepted the invitation) to speak at another, co-ed event for students interested in a finance career. I asked the Human Resources team how they had achieved this transformation. They explained that a detailed study of the applications showed that the female students tended to apply later than the men. No one knew why, but instead of disputing the finding or wasting valuable time investigating, the recruitment team simply accepted the need to take this into account. They devised a new approach for accepting candidates, holding back a number of places until applications closed, so there was enough room for promising female students applying near the deadline. At the same time, they had broadened their outreach to more universities, although they still felt there was more work to do here. Overall, the team had made very significant changes in their own long-established process and achieved a real breakthrough.

Importantly, they were delighted with the quality of their 2016 interns and observed that their greater diversity had really made a positive impact on the way they had worked together on assignments.

Andy Haldane, Chief Economist at the Bank of England, gave an insightful speech on diversity in 2016, entitled 'The Sneetches', after Dr Seuss' children's story of the same name, a parody of status and discrimination first published in 1961. In his speech, Haldane challenged CEOs to consider whether their recruitment process really did encourage diversity.

Andy Haldane's Recruitment Challenge

There are two candidates for a position, A and B. They do a test based on the attributes useful for the hiring organisation. These tests might be state of the art, including all of the diverse attributes one would wish for in an organisation – cognitive, interpersonal and experiential skills.

In this test out of 10, candidate A scores 8 and candidate B scores 4. Which one should be hired? The answer is easy. The evidence points strongly to A as the candidate best meeting the requirements for the job. They have, quite literally, ticked the right boxes. But let's add a twist. What if the answers A gets wrong are the ones B gets right? And what if the questions existing employees get wrong are also the ones B gets right? In

---

other words, what if candidate B brings skills to the organisation which otherwise do not exist?

The right recruitment decision for the organisation is then to choose B rather than A. Candidate B adds more to the collective ability of the organisation, even though they are weaker individually. The question is, how often would existing recruitment practices deliver such an outcome? In practice, I think rarely. Individuals are typically judged on the alignment between their skills and those of the existing organisation. It takes quite a leap of faith to choose instead the candidate whose skills are misaligned with the hiring organisation.

When it's set out like this, everyone can see that candidate B is the candidate who adds something new to the organisation. I have cited this challenge many times and on every occasion, those in the room are shocked by how obvious it is and yet how their own recruitment process would not lead to the 'right' candidate, B, being offered the role. We still think in terms of hiring the 'best' individual, *not the best person to complete the team*. We need to put the hire, the promotion, and the choice of someone to do a particular task in the context of the whole group. This requires many companies – and that means their CEOs – to tear up their rulebook: hiring is not about finding 'another one' like those you have, but deliberately seeking out difference. It's not something that comes especially easily: I've been guilty of cloning myself, selecting two student interns one summer who were in many respects (much) younger versions of myself (one was even called Helena). We got on really well, of course, but I hadn't intended to make the mistake of hiring echo chambers – so the next year I consciously sought interns with vastly different backgrounds and ways of thinking to my own. I learned as much from them as (I hope) they did from me. As more recruiters start to grasp this, individuals from under-represented areas have an obvious advantage, with their differences being inherently valuable, rather than an impediment.

Intuitively, this is an area where artificial intelligence could really help us to overcome our natural biases – but only of course if we use AI specifically to identify those candidates who offer the skills we are currently missing. At present, undergraduates tell me that much of the programmed screening appears designed to perpetuate the conventional definition of 'good'. They mention, too, that video interviews where no human interviewer is involved – and instead the candidate has a couple of minutes to answer each question in front of a camera – suit some applicants but that others find them disconcerting. Recruitment processes that are inherently adaptable to suit diverse personalities are surely essential if we are really to widen the talent pool. As artificial intelligence improves, no doubt we can also refine its application, but at present there seems more danger of standardising approaches further and mistaking lack of human intervention for less bias. Again, it's understandable to latch on to new methods as we seek to improve the flawed approaches of the past, but we need to be prepared to question them. There should be nothing sacrosanct about an idea just because we are trying it out in the name of diversity.

From mentoring to tutorials

Mentoring is popular in many organisations, and I have seen it being most effective when a two-way relationship develops between mentor and mentee. There's a separate debate about mentoring versus 'sponsorship', where the sponsor actively champions the more junior person's career, which is fabulous, but it is hard to find a sponsor until you are already quite established. Mentoring is more accessible and usually focused on career advice; the concept can easily be extended to bring diverse (in any sense) pairs together to work on business ideas or problems. As an undergraduate, I benefited from weekly tutorials, a cornerstone of the teaching method at Cambridge and some other universities. Tutorials are not one-way conversations; the pupil or undergraduate writes the essay, of course, and the 'don' critiques it but the tutorial itself is a discussion, where ideas flow both ways. These rich conversations can enlighten both pupil and teacher. The tutorial format can be replicated in a business environment: regular, scheduled and frequent (say, weekly) dialogues between two employees at different levels of seniority to work on a project or business challenge. In this way, both parties can develop a greater understanding of different points of view and the advantages of listening to each other. In a world of great and rapid transformations, particularly around technology, creating opportunities for senior staff (in both age and hierarchy) to listen to those closer to the vanguard of change has many benefits besides fostering diversity.

One of the 30% Club programmes that has had the biggest impact is a cross-company mentoring scheme for mid-career women. It doesn't sound terribly exciting and when accounting and consultancy firm EY first suggested it, I was doubtful – surely the world did not need yet another mentoring scheme? In typical 30% Club fashion, we tested out the idea through a pilot, involving just eight companies and 70 people, 35 mentors and 35 mentees. The feedback was illuminating. The male mentors said that the conversations had 'opened their eyes' to the issues women in their own company must be facing but either didn't have the opportunity to raise or weren't comfortable discussing with colleagues. (Male mentors also received some of the most enthusiastic reviews: the first 'Mentor of the Year' award, following the 'class of 2016/17', went to my former colleague Michael Cole-Fontayn, then European Chair of BNY Mellon.) The mentees confirmed they felt able to be more candid in these conversations with someone outside their own firm – and that the advice was less restrained, too. The feedback from the fourth cohort shows the positive impact of these frank exchanges: 95% of mentees reported that their confidence as a leader had grown as a result of their mentoring and 86% of mentors reported that they had gained learning from their mentoring experience. It may be difficult to fully replicate this candour within a business, but tutorials can help build understanding and mutual respect.

Give innovative thinkers the stage

The 30% Club mentoring pilot (which became an annual programme, growing rapidly each year – the sixth cohort involves over 100 organisations and nearly 2,500 people) also showed that mentees wanted to hear bigger, bolder, inspiring ideas from speakers beyond the corporate world. This might have been a challenge for me to arrange, but out of the blue I received a letter from Theresa May, then Home Secretary and Minister for Women and Equalities. Mrs May asked if I would meet one of her constituents, Liz Dimmock, as she thought we might be able to help one another.

Liz is an impressive woman. Formerly Global Head of Coaching at HSBC, in 2012 she also cycled the Tour de Force, the entire Tour de France course, a week ahead of the race (women are still not allowed to officially compete in the flagship race). Liz recognised that businesswomen and sportswomen could learn a lot from each other and founded a social enterprise to encourage that through mentoring: Women Ahead. We met and I realised just how much Liz and her team could add to the nascent 30%

Club scheme – including sourcing exciting speakers from the worlds of sport, art and entertainment. Not only could these speakers inspire mentees, they would expose mentors, often very senior executives, to fresh ideas.

One particular event stands out for me: a mesmerising talk by voice coach Patsy Rodenburg, whose clients are mainly well-known actors (such as Orlando Bloom), on how to command both a room and a conversation. Patsy had asked if she could speak to the group for two hours: conscious that we had a lot of senior people in the room and doubtful that anyone could hold our attention that long, I limited her to 90 minutes, but regretted that. As I looked out at the 400-strong audience, I could see that everyone – man and woman, mentor and mentee – was hanging on her every word. Patsy made us all think differently about how we engage with our colleagues, friends and family, how we can be more present and powerful in our conversations. I have undertaken many 'presentation skills' courses but all in the context of corporate training. None were as helpful as Patsy's insights. Again, CEOs can encourage more innovative thinking in their own organisations by inviting in charismatic speakers beyond the 'usual' roster. (If access to these talks is linked to mentoring or tutorial programmes, that might be an additional incentive for more people to get involved.) Business leaders can also give the stage to internal orators to share their 'blue sky' thinking, giving people the licence to come forward with their ideas. A programme that deliberately cultivates and celebrates new thinking is a simple design evolution and one that can have many positive second-order effects. It shows an openness of mind, a willingness to listen to new concepts that may challenge the status quo.

These are just a few examples of practical changes that can help CEOs press the diversity reset button, to encourage people to think anew about the issue of broadening talent at all levels. Making all roles open to agile working (not part-time but doing the work with minimal constraints), advertising new positions under the banner 'happy to talk flexible working', and promoting returnships – bridges back into work for those who've had a career break – are three other 'radical' (not really) ideas. The various suggestions can be grouped together under a task force – but the issue shouldn't be outsourced to Human Resources, or even to an executive sponsor. These resources can certainly help, including with 'project management', but it's very important that CEOs are directly engaged. A CEO's job is demanding but we can all find time to do the things that matter. It sends a very strong signal when a CEO is personally involved in mentoring, in tutorials, in attending some of the 'innovative thinker' speaking events, in interviewing 'left field' job candidates and promoting those who work flexibly.

Experimentation is key. Most businesses don't experiment adventurously when it comes to their own organisational structures and working practices. This is unsurprising (the hassle! – and the inevitable, more immediate priorities) but if the goal is genuine improvement and nothing has worked so far, the starting point must be an open mind. Newer companies are able to start the way they mean to go on – I heard a presentation from the founder of a successful investment company, whose first twelve employees boasted nine different first languages between them. (He admitted this ultra-diversity made communication hard in the early days.)

I'm frequently asked for extra ideas to help sectors that are particularly male-dominated – such as technology, engineering or finance. First, we need to be honest with ourselves about how much of the imbalance is cultural (and can be addressed) and how much might be down to men and women's differing levels of interest (on average) in these fields. The goal is not to pressure girls into careers that they might not be especially interested in but which are portrayed as 'superior' to those they actually might enjoy. (That seems to me to undermine women rather than boost us.) But if a girl does love physics or maths (the first-ever female winner of the prestigious Fields Medal was announced in 2014, an Iranian mathematician, Maryam Mirzakhani, who sadly died of breast cancer three years later aged just 40) then we need to ensure that she perceives that she can fulfil her potential – and for the reality to match that perception.

Image is an additional problem for companies in these industries: absent a concerted, sector-wide effort, it's very hard to change general impressions that may adversely impact recruitment. As we've already seen, technology companies are amongst the most challenged, particularly when it comes to attracting female engineers, but they have confronted the criticism and a potentially vicious spiral directly by publishing their adverse data, saying it's not good enough and committing to keep publishing to show whether they are improving.

Different sectors face different challenges. In 2012, a number of the managing partners of professional services firms – lawyers, accountants and management consultants – asked the 30% Club for help. These firms are usually able to attract plenty of women at entry level – often more than half their intake – but struggle to achieve anything approaching gender balance at partnership level (at the time, female partners were 15% of the law firm average, 17% at accountancies). They hoped that collectively, under what they termed the 'safe harbour' of the 30% Club, they might be able to achieve the breakthrough that had eluded them all individually.

Looking across ten legal and seven accountancy firms, we found that a man was *ten times* more likely to make partner at a law firm than a woman who had joined at the same time; three times more likely at accountancy firms. This was despite these firms 'doing a lot' to address the issue: most could show me long lists of specific initiatives aimed at developing their female talent, and some had been working on the issue for many years.

In a special project for the 30% Club, McKinsey surveyed over 700 people across these firms. They found a big gap between what the managing partners were saying about the importance of diversity and the commitment of even those who reported directly to them. Three-quarters of managing partners considered diversity to be a strategic priority. When asked anonymously, only 40% of senior partners and 25% of managers expressed a similar view. The lack of real commitment amongst those who were managing lots of people was an obvious impediment.

It was also a tough message for the managing partners, but as one of them put it, 'we needed to know: this is a tipping point'. For them, it had become about sustainable success, about profits. Those at the top could see clients demanding more diversity: 'We've entered pitches with an all-male team to come across a team with 50% women on the client's side and faced an adverse reaction.' It was already becoming hard to attract even traditional top talent: 'Unless we can solve this, we won't be able to attract and retain the best and the brightest young men *or* young women.'

Those UK-based professional services firms who asked the 30% Club for help did set and *publish* voluntary targets for female partners, while making clear design changes to modernise their working practices. Some were quite rudimentary: in 2012, we discovered that only a third of these firms had proper work allocation processes. At the others, the best projects – the ones that would help set associates on the path to promotion – tended to be given out by partners to people who were, well, junior versions of themselves. Introducing a robust work allocation process was a simple first step. Some of the firms have gone further, reviewing business models to move away from the outdated billable hours system so that they measure output rather than input, and managing their talented women in a 'gender intelligent' way.

Those design changes have had a demonstrable impact: McKinsey's follow-up review in 2015 showed that men were now 'only' three times more likely than women to be promoted to partner at law firms. In the best cases – the proportion of female partners appointed at one major law firm was a record 40% in 2017 – progress has been achieved by many people doing many things differently. These firms are now measuring and managing their talent pipelines much more closely, carefully preparing women for the next stage towards partnership rather than waiting until they may have missed a step. They work harder at 'closing the deal' when women hesitate. One accountancy firm told me that they had offered partnership to two high-performing women, and had been shocked when both turned the offer down. Rather than leave it there, a senior female colleague invited each separately to a meeting and discovered that both were pregnant with their first child and anxious about the firm's expectations if they accepted the promotion. Both were encouraged to accept – and did – with the reassurance that if they wanted to work fewer hours that would be fine. The women said they were pleased the intervention was made, and were happy that they were persuaded to change their minds.

My own industry, the investment and savings profession, is a latecomer to the diversity agenda and our statistics are terrible – not only in the UK but globally. Citywire analyses the numbers of women managing money around the world, based on the fund managers in its extensive database. Its 2018 report covered 16,084 active managers: just 1,662 (10.3%) are female – and it turns out that even this overstates things: only 6.2% of funds are managed solely by a woman. Yet I am testament to the fact that fund management can be a great career not just for women with families, but for anyone who wants to be judged on results rather than hours at the desk. The industry has, if anything, gone backwards since the financial crisis – the image issue has become an even bigger obstacle. In 2016, as chair of the Investment Association, the UK's industry trade body, I hosted a breakfast round table to discuss what we should do about the situation. I asked the 40 attendees, all senior at their respective firms, to submit a short biography, not in the usual glittering prizes format but along lines that captured their personal characteristics and backgrounds. Mine read:

I am white British, went to a co-ed comprehensive school, then to Cambridge where I read Philosophy, joined Schroders straight from University on their graduate programme, was a fixed income fund analyst for them in New York, returned to London as a fixed income fund manager before moving to Newton in 1994. I was CEO of Newton from 2001–2016 and am now leading a new venture, Personal Investing, for Legal and General Investment Management. I am married, my husband and I have nine children and he is a stay-at-home dad.

Reading the compilation, which showed a wide range of educational attainment levels and many experimental early careers, we agreed that few of us would make it through our own, more formulaic recruitment processes today. Many firms were stipulating a Maths, Finance or Economics degree, for example. The breakfast led to the Diversity Project, an intense, collaborative effort to improve industry diversity across *all* its dimensions.

I'm frequently asked if businesses should target gender first or whether it's better to address multiple aspects of diversity all at once. I believe there was a time and a place for the 30% Club's razor-like focus on gender; newer initiatives, like the Diversity Project, should be more holistic from the start. That doesn't equate to a generalised, vague (and therefore doomed) attempt to achieve progress – we still need targeted actions – but broader diversity goals can actually be more effective for women's advancement than 'just gender'. A male colleague told me (not so very long ago), 'I don't know why you focus on women so much, they've never had it so good,' revealing a great deal about his personal feelings regarding all the recent attention paid to female talent.

I'm certainly conscious that this attention may have made it harder for companies to work out how to address those other dimensions. At one point, the idea of a 20% target for ethnic minority board directors was mooted in the UK, which initially sounds promising, but what about LGBTQ+ representation? Disability? The 30% Club's numeric target was helpful as a means of addressing one source of under-representation but extending the exact same approach quickly feels problematic. Diversifying talent is about wanting more ideas, to open up the pool of talent, not to manufacture a pop band. Ultimately, we want diversity of thought, and that takes a subtler approach than 'three women, two ethnic minority, one gay, one disabled, one young, etc.'. *How can we find solutions for the 100%?*

Mellody Hobson is an accomplished African-American businesswoman and non-executive board director. She is a driving force behind efforts to improve the representation of black directors on boards of American companies, currently around 9% on Fortune 500 companies, compared with 13% of the population. Less than 1% of CEOs of the same Fortune 500 companies are black – there are just three today and since Ursula Burns stepped down as the CEO of Xerox Corporation, none of them are women. Burns is, to date, the only African-American woman to have *ever* led a Fortune 500 company.

Mellody invited me to speak at the 2016 Black National Corporate Directors conference in California and interviewed me alongside a (white, male) Fortune 500 CEO. The CEO had analysed his company's customer base and found that two-thirds were *not* white men. Instead of addressing 'just' gender, or race, they were working towards approximating this two-thirds 'other' within the company's board and management team. There was continued support for initiatives focusing on specific under-represented groups, but the overall goal was to reduce the dominance of the unrepresentative white male leadership. This approach is not just appealingly holistic but a powerful reminder that the 'other' forms the majority.

Finally, let's talk frankly about the complex issues facing female CEOs in promoting diversity. We have seen how the male chairmen had a transformative impact in improving the gender balance in Britain's boardrooms. But even now, when senior men have become so much more involved, few women at the top seem completely comfortable playing a leading role. Those who do can be hugely inspirational: Alison Brittain, CEO of Whitbread, gave a brilliant address at the *Financial Times* 'Women at the Top' conference in 2016. She shared her experience of making the move from managing director at a bank to a FTSE-100 CEO at Britain's largest hospitality company. Alison explained that, as a new CEO, she had underestimated the impact that her every remark, even her mood, would have on her team. She overheard a colleague say, 'She doesn't look very happy, I don't think she liked our presentation' as they left the room; in fact, Alison was looking glum because she had suddenly remembered her daughter's maths homework and was trying to recall how to do quadratic equations.

In sharing her stories, Alison showed her humanity, making her – for me – a real role model. Her willingness to stand up as a female CEO is, however, far from the norm. Others are more ambivalent; not, it seems, because they don't want to encourage other women but because they do not want to be 'seen to be flying the women's flag' (a direct quote from a FTSE-100 female executive). There is a view that 'real businesswomen' should be focusing on 'real business issues', rather than on women – but of course these are part of the same agenda. I understand the anxiety – I have felt it myself. But by being in any way reticent, female business leaders perpetuate the notion that gender equality is still a special interest topic – or, just as bad, that it's a career risk to champion other women. Those who have stepped up should be celebrated; so my friend Suki Sandhu, founder of the OUTstanding and EMpower lists – recognising gay and ethnic minority executive role models respectively – and I have worked with the *Financial Times* to create a new list of 'HERoes' to do just that. 'HERoes' is not a 'power list' as such – those on it have many impressive career achievements, but the clinching criterion is that they have encouraged the progression of other women. Melanie Richards, vice chair of KPMG in the UK, ranked number one on the inaugural list, is a wonderful example of someone who has worked hard on behalf of others over many years – often behind the scenes.

I would love to see more female CEOs taking steps to change working practices – yes, to be more female-friendly, but also to ensure that the next generation of both men and women can work smarter. Mary Portas has done just that. Portas is a retailing expert and broadcaster – her TV programmes, including *Mary Queen of Shops*, and her charitable Living and Giving campaign have made her a household name in the UK. She suddenly realised after the birth of Horatio, her third child and the first with her wife, Melanie Rickey (Portas was previously married to a man), that work wasn't making her happy. After more than twenty years building up a successful business she tore up her own rulebook and decided to create a working life that she – and others – would enjoy. In a 2017 interview she set out the new rules: she would no longer work with people she did not like, she would be home by 6 p.m. – and as many people as possible who worked for her would be able to do the same. She said: 'I realised how much of my life had been spent working and being treated like a man. Even the way I was presented on TV fitted that profile – I was supposed to be "scary, ball-breaking" – but deep inside I knew I wasn't like that.'

The catalyst for Mary's new approach was thinking about her own life. But as her interviewer, Margarette Driscoll, pointed out, Mary Portas has built a highly successful career on spotting trends. She has now reshaped her company around smart ways of working. Her top staff set their own hours, take open-ended maternity leave, and as much holiday as they like. Portas points out, 'This isn't just about women, I've got two men and two women on my board and the men love it. This is how men want to work, too.' Portas believes that, 'given freedom, people work smarter – and harder'. If they can choose how much time they take off, 'people actually spend less time away'.

This is borne out by the experience of market-leading entertainment company Netflix. Since 2010, Netflix's holiday policy has been … to have no policy at all. Salaried employees can take as much time off as they'd like. The company focuses on what people get done, not how many hours or days they work. Autonomy makes people more accountable, not less. I don't think it's a coincidence that companies like Netflix, which set their own agenda based on what works rather than what we have been used to, have enjoyed a meteoric rise.

I believe the word 'leapfrog' is going to become familiar in the business world, as in Netflix 'leapfrogs Disney to become the most valuable media company in the world'. We have only seen the start of the battle between disrupters and disrupted (with the latter often fighting back with their own innovations, and a constant influx of new challengers). There is certainly no hiding place for long-established brands as innovators create new, exciting and relevant products and services – and ways of working that attract the best staff. In my view, three characteristics will be essential to win: smart use of technology, alignment with customers' needs and values, and fostering creative, diverse teams.

We've covered a lot of ground, so here's a short checklist for CEOs who want results:

1. Analyse your data and listen – yourself – to the experiences of both the under-represented and 'traditional talent'. Encourage honesty. Don't speculate.
2. Accept the results, say what you're going to do to improve things, set out timelines and milestones. Tear up the action plan that hasn't worked.

3. Aim to create voluntary buy-in to the project at all levels and involving the majority group. Drop the 'D-word' if necessary.

4. Make HR one of the most important areas of the business, right next to you, headed by a star. Talent, both individual and collective, is integral to strategy. Seek to create a talent ecosystem.

5. Consider every stage of the career life cycle and set goals with rewards for achievement (carrots, not sticks).

6. Make design changes that work for your company around recruitment, promotion, pay. Think in terms of the whole team, keep resisting the temptation to consider each role in isolation. Create more opportunities for varied talent to work together. Invite unusual speakers in to catalyse new thinking. Consider making every job open to *agile* or *smart* working. (Drop the 'flexible' tag too if it seems to carry stigma.)

7. Advertise what you are doing, internally and externally, making clear that your objective is real diversity of thought, not merely the appearance of change. Walk the talk. Mellody Hobson, married to *Star Wars* creator George Lucas, quotes Yoda: 'Do or do not, there is no try.'

8. Repeat step 1 and sustain the effort until it's no longer needed – and enjoy reaping a diversity dividend.

Chapter 7

Own the process

Nearly all successful people begin with two beliefs:
1. The future can be better than the present
2. I have the power to make it so

DAVID BROOKS, *NEW YORK TIMES*, QUOTED BY VALA
AFSHAR, CHIEF DIGITAL EVANGELIST, SALESFORCE

OK, so you're not quite a CEO yet. Perhaps you're still at school or university, just starting out on your career, or trying to work out how to take that very first step between the worlds of education and work. The previous chapter may have worried you: if diversity is now such a sensitive topic, if CEOs are still figuring it out, how can it be such a good time to be a girl?

While it's important to be aware that the world of work isn't quite 'fixed' yet – otherwise you might fall at the first hurdle – it's also important to realise that you can help create the conditions for your own success, *whatever* your circumstances. 'Getting your head in the game' – being in the right frame of mind to explore your own potential, to take chances and then make the most of them (including picking yourself up and trying again, if necessary) – is the starting point. Please note, this is not a call to be aggressive. It's a call to be *open to possibilities* – and then to own the process around making the most of them.

I have had a number of mentees, from a wide range of socio-economic, educational, ethnic, religious and cultural backgrounds. Each has faced distinct challenges, including – for some – a big gulf between their own ambitions and their parents' expectations. Several have taken a bold and controversial step to embark on a career at all; one refused to enter into an arranged marriage, another, still in her twenties, is constantly under pressure to start a family. A third, the mother of two, is struggling to develop a shared partnership with her husband around their family, although she is the one with the higher earnings and career potential. All these young women have skills, strong personalities, and high aspirations. How can they reconcile these conflicts, let alone develop their focus?

At the start of each relationship, we've worked together to develop clearer goals. They've all – like me – started off with rather vague ideas about what personal success looks like, so I've asked each one to fast-forward five years: what version of her future self would make the mentee feel happy and fulfilled? It's a revealing exercise: one young woman wrote 'being married' right at the very top of her list and told me she had never even admitted that to herself before. Up until that point, she had thought of herself as first and foremost a 'career woman', and having made great sacrifices to get where she was, was surprised to realise that progressing further in her career did *not* feature in her priorities. It was clear that she needed to rebalance her life – as well as reignite her enthusiasm for her work. (You may be surprised that I did not in any way try to change her mind – far from it. Progress isn't about being forced down a specific path. It's about having more scope to live the life you want.)

When we're in the midst of our own life, it's not always easy to accurately assess the way our priorities are changing. Taking time to step back from the day-to-day, to consciously assess and then reassess what's important to us now helps us see the right next steps. When I left Newton after so many years, I wasn't at all sure of my next move, and needed both time and space to reflect. I also knew what made me happy at work. Being able to do a good job while also trying to improve society – to combine profit with purpose – was when I felt most fulfilled, most able to be 'myself' and in turn most likely to perform well. That, career-wise at least, was my definition of success.

If you're right at the start, or feeling very unsure about what your own version of success looks like, stop and think for a moment about something you have done that has made you feel proud of yourself. It could be something that other people might not think of as particularly special, or it could be something very obviously 'big': the key is to recognise that feeling of achievement, the distinct awareness that you overcame an obstacle or exceeded your own expectations. A sense of accomplishment that rarely comes when we are gifted an easy path.

This is the feeling to aim for as you look to develop from where you are today. Note that it probably involves taking some risk. It's really difficult to make much progress if we stay inside our comfort zone. But even a small step beyond starts to expand our frontiers, and if we take enough of those small steps, we can grow much more than any of us might think possible. If anyone had said to me when I was a shy and gawky teenager that one day I would have nine children *and* be the chief executive of an investment company *and* work on initiatives to drive gender equality, I would have laughed (nervously).

Of course, those things happened over time, not in one fell swoop. When I told my boss that I was pregnant with my seventh child, he offered his hearty congratulations but from the look on his face I could see that he was unsure what it meant for the business. I tried to reassure him by pointing out that my family wasn't going from 'nought to seven children all at once'. He smiled, and replied, 'That's a good way of thinking about it, in fact it's just a 17% increase.' I might not have put it quite like that, but taking things one at a time – including, in our family, one baby at a time – has been an important part of not just coping but expanding to meet the challenges as they have grown.

I don't mind when people are curious about how I 'do it all' (by now it should be obvious that the answer is 'with help' – not so much paid help as lots of input from others), but it makes me uncomfortable when I'm labelled a 'super-woman'. For a start, I don't feel 'super' most of the time, I feel very human, with all the uncertainties and failings that come with our condition. More importantly, the description might discourage others by implying that certain goals are unobtainable. The truth is, I am just an ordinary girl from an ordinary background, not the cleverest or the most talented amongst any group of peers. I am not saying that to be modest; all I have really done is to stretch myself, little by little, beyond what is regarded as the norm – and beyond my comfort zone. I'm also very persistent. As my boss alluded to when considering the news of my seventh child, each incremental change has looked quite feasible, even if the overall big picture is rather less so. I have learned to concentrate on that immediate next step. It's been an important factor in my life as well as my career, and not just because of the 'volumes' of children or daily tasks, 'bigness' of jobs and so on. The compound effect of a series of small actions can be huge – either positively or negatively. Tiny differences in girls' education compared with boys', as we'll explore shortly, can accumulate to create a meaningful – adverse – gap when it comes to being ready for the workplace. The minor deviations that as women we often take away from the career curve of our male colleagues, each barely perceptible, similarly add up over time until suddenly we are noticeably behind. The good news is, we can avoid or correct these individually small divergences.

Over many years, as I have gradually pushed out my own boundaries it's become clearer to me that our feelings of limitations are often self-imposed, or relative to standards set by others. Fabled investor Warren Buffett wrote a wonderful essay for *Fortune* magazine about the imbalance between his opportunities growing up and those of his sisters – simply because he was a boy. He put it so succinctly: 'my floor became my sisters' ceiling'. Now, he said, 'thank heavens, the structural barriers are falling, but still an obstacle remains: too many women continue to impose limitations on themselves, talking themselves out of achieving their potential'. Referring to a friend, the late Katharine Graham, who lacked self-belief, he said he had told her to 'discard the funhouse mirror that others had set before her and instead view herself in a mirror that reflected reality, a reality that was a match for anyone, male or female'. I have never met Mr Buffett but in a 'taking a chance' frame of mind, I once wrote to him, inviting him to become a member of the fledgling US chapter of the 30% Club. To my amazement, he wrote straight back, explaining how important he thought gender balance was, how he was aiming for this over the medium term for the board of Berkshire Hathaway and the embarrassment he felt in telling a mother of nine that he wouldn't have much time to devote but was happy to lend his support. He then added a lovely handwritten 'PS', saying he had heard I was 'terrific'. That was one of those exciting moments, when I realised that the 30% Club idea was now influencing the influencers.

I've come to see that such moments, while infrequent, are far more likely to occur when I've 'owned the process', rather than leaned in to someone else's agenda.

In the midst of the 2018 World Cup campaign, England football manager Gareth Southgate revealed that he was training his players to 'own the process' when it came to penalty shoot-outs (England's Achilles heel at big tournaments). Southgate channelled lessons learned from his own missed penalty in the Euro '96 semi-final match between Germany and England when, as the 'sixth man', he had not expected to be asked to take a penalty. Southgate ensured that his players were prepared for the eventuality – right down to the twenty-third man. Each player was encouraged to formulate their own plan, to write their own story, to see being called up to take a penalty as an opportunity and to approach the big moment calmly. That conscious strategy yielded a semi-final place for the England team, the first in twenty-eight years. In press interviews, Southgate also revealed much about his own journey since Euro '96: 'I've learnt a million things from the day and the years that have followed it … the biggest thing being that when something goes wrong in your life, it doesn't finish you.'

Gareth Southgate's leadership skills have rightly been praised – and widely recognised as applicable way beyond the football field. While the 2018 World Cup tournament was still underway, I had the opportunity to meet a talented young American woman, Jillian Ross, whose mother Ann had dialled in to the Brian Lehrer New York radio show when I was being interviewed. On air, Ann mentioned that her 19-year-old daughter was interning at a London-based asset management boutique. I was keen to meet Jillian and am so glad I did. Her major at Columbia is brilliant enough: Computer Science and Philosophy. What could possibly top that? Her tale of running for student president at her co-ed high school. The first step involved an election speech for the class president vote, at the age of fourteen. All the other candidates were boys, and they spoke before her. Their speeches were light-hearted and jokey, and by the time it was Jillian's turn, she had decided her serious, prepared speech was a mistake. She made an impromptu attempt to lean in to what seemed the route to success, but her bad jokes bombed and she didn't get elected. The following year, Jillian stuck to what she was really all about, owning the process – and won, so (slightly belatedly) starting her journey to becoming over-all student president in her final year.

Of course, 'owning the process' is often easier said than done. For a start, many of us *do* suffer from distorted, unflattering visions of ourselves. Those crazy mirrors, like the ones at funfairs, *do* exist in our minds. In these situations, we need to make a deliberate attempt to 'fake it until we make it' (which less catchily is really 'consciously correcting our self-undermining tendencies until we make it'). You don't need to actually *feel* confident, but you need to *appear* confident. If you seem to believe in yourself, it makes others more likely to believe in you too, and that really does have a confidence-boosting effect. Eventually, no 'faking' is required.

In 2012, Amy Cuddy gave a brilliant TED talk on how our body language can actually make us who we are. Most of us would agree with the notion that our mind can influence our body; Amy showed that our body can influence our mind. She set out the evidence that 'power posing' – for just two minutes before an important interview or presentation – can make our testosterone levels rise and our cortisol levels fall (those hormones again) – creating a more confident, more 'winning' version of ourselves.

Cuddy had watched classes of business school students and noticed that some people were 'caricatures of alphas', occupying the middle of the classroom, 'sort of spreading out', whereas others were 'virtually collapsing' as they came into the room, and that those differences were related to gender. Women tended to shrink, men to expand (I see this all the time). At the same time, business schools were struggling with a gender grade gap; men and women came into MBA courses equally well qualified but women got lower grades at the end. Much of the gap was attributable to the women participating less in class, so Cuddy started to explore whether it was possible to get them to *mimic* the confidence they needed to participate more.

The evidence from her experiments, where people were told to adopt certain physical poses and were then subjected to a tough job interview, was compelling enough – it turns out that adopting the 'Wonder Woman' pose for just two minutes as *preparation* for an important performance (not on stage itself!) enables us to act most powerfully.

The clincher, though, was Cuddy's own life story. At the age of nineteen, she was involved in a bad car crash, suffering a head injury that adversely impacted her IQ and, with it, her self-esteem. Eventually, four years after her peers, she graduated from college and then, with the help of an 'angel adviser', Susan Fiske, went to Princeton. Her first challenge was to give a 20-minute talk to fellow students. The night before, she called Susan and said she

The Wonder Woman power pose

couldn't do it, that she wasn't supposed to be there, that she was an impostor. Her confidante told her, 'You are going to fake it. You're going to do every talk that you ever get asked to do. You're just going to do it and do it and do it … until you have this moment where you say, "Oh my gosh, I'm doing it, like I have *become* this."' What was especially wonderful about this story was that Amy then described how she recognised a fellow student was suffering from the same (misplaced) lack of self-belief and was able to help her in a similar way.

Much less dramatically, I have experienced a similar evolution, from being terrified about standing up on stage to really enjoying it. I used to feel physically sick before a big presentation, and that inevitably detracted from my performances. I couldn't channel the adrenalin to be effective. The first time I appeared on live TV my eyes were visibly twitching. The only cure was to keep performing. I now (mostly) look forward to those big moments, seeing them as opportunities to communicate, to draw more people into my ideas, to gauge their reactions and learn from them. The turning point was when I moved my emphasis from thinking about how *I* felt, to starting from the *audience's* perspective. What did I have to say that might really resonate with each person? What would enable them to *enjoy* the talk, to absorb the ideas rather than merely listen politely? Through trial and error, I learned I needed to talk without notes to get real audience engagement – I still needed to write out the speech so the structure and content were there, but then throw those notes away. It was not a coincidence that at that point I moved from being an OK-ish presenter to a sought-after one. (I still mess up from time to time, but now see those as learning experiences, not a reason to hide away. I also still get nervous when pushing out my own frontiers – in 2015 I felt honoured to be asked to be a keynote speaker at the Women's Institute's wonderful 100th anniversary event at the Royal Albert Hall, but as I looked out from the 'wings' at the capacity crowd of over five thousand, it was hard not to run).

I have observed much the same pattern in others. I had seen a young analyst present to colleagues on several occasions and thought she would be a great speaker at our annual client seminar. Initially she reacted enthusiastically, but she came to see me the next day and told me she felt anxious. She had never presented onstage before, she didn't know if she would be able to pull it off and was afraid of letting everyone down. While she was grateful for the opportunity, perhaps, she suggested, I should ask someone else? I asked if she might be prepared to give it a go, said that we would ensure she had plenty of training and practice, and if she continued to feel very nervous she could pull out, right up to the day before – I would have a back-up plan. Having gone through many more hours of training than her colleagues, including a word-perfect rehearsal, she was – of course – the star of the show. When I congratulated her afterwards, she thanked me for not letting her turn the chance down. She had pushed herself beyond her comfort zone and learned new skills. Over the following months and years, she became one of the firm's most highly respected presenters.

In recent years, I have also had the opportunity to see some ultra-powerful people – including prime ministers, government ministers, CEOs and others with great influence – up close. They are exposed to performance situations that most people would crumble just thinking about. While they have become practised at delivering, often flawlessly, I have seen them in the wings. I can report that everyone has vulnerabilities, coping mechanisms, allies and support systems. Even those who blithely say 'I never get nervous' have rituals before they go onstage. In many ways, they are just like you and me – wanting validation, still feeling vulnerable as human beings. In a radio interview, Sir Paul McCartney revealed fellow Beatle John Lennon's insecurities – before mentioning that he himself avoids reading reviews: 'You should never do it because the next day you're going to have go and do something, you're going to play somewhere and you just go in and think "I'm no good", because this guy thinks I'm no good.' McCartney acknowledged, 'It's pathetic, it really is. I know a lot of people who are famous and have done loads of great things and it is common.'

We all need a confidante (or two). With their encouragement, you still won't (can't) know *for sure* whether you can achieve something new but you needn't be paralysed by anxiety. You will start to see that it's OK to be vulnerable – in fact it's part of how we grow, as we embrace those new opportunities.

I've mentioned my daughter Clara before. Clara is a beautiful spirit, one of the most giving people I have ever known. She is also very indecisive (we ask her to pre-read menus online even when we are just going out for pizza, to help her – and us – when it comes to ordering). She was unsure about whether to go on to art college when she finished academic school, so for many months we held up that reality-check mirror, to help her see how others (not just her family) perceive her talent, and to experiment with different courses that might help her decide. She took an art course at a well-known college, and was surprised that the other students all expressed uncertainty about their future. 'I didn't realise other people weren't sure either.' With help, hopefully Clara was eventually able to see that at 17, even if she was making the 'wrong' decision, if she lost a year by taking a misstep, that would make little difference in the long term. The experience of trying something to see if she enjoyed it was all she needed to focus on as she learned to own the process around her future.

A shortage of money can limit our ability to experiment, of course, but we might still be able to test how much we really want something. As the daughter of teachers, my first career choice – becoming a barrister – wasn't really one I could easily entertain, as it would have involved several more years of little or no earnings after university. Nevertheless, I was able to find ways to see how much I really wanted to work around these financial constraints – I did a 'mini-pupillage' for a week and was also able to try a short law course in the holidays. The good news was that those experiences were enough for me to know that the law wasn't my calling.

It's pretty obvious that if you enjoy something you are much more likely to be good at it. University was a much happier experience than school for me, partly because my degree subject – Philosophy – attracted a wide range of students. I had a mixed circle of friends, not only by gender but by background, sexuality and ethnicity. Philosophy also proved to be just what my 18-year-old self needed, sweeping away my lazy assumptions, requiring a disciplined way of approaching problems and encouraging lateral thinking. Philosophy is a great equaliser: no one has the answers but everyone can contribute to the evolution of the ideas. All that really matters is to be logical. The discipline helped me never to take things at face value and not to be afraid of challenging the consensus. Philosophy is not widely regarded as a good choice when it comes to employability – in fact, when I was applying, my parents showed me a newspaper article ranking degrees according to employment prospects: philosophy came right at the bottom. But I was really interested in the subject, and my parents respected that, an approach that Richard and I have definitely taken with our own children. We are all diverse: it is wonderful to find a talent or a subject that excites you, and to be encouraged to develop that interest as far as you can, including reaching for the next goals. Whatever you do, don't choose a subject that doesn't interest you just because it seems to lead to an obvious 'safe' career – the chances are you won't feel much interest in the job, either.

So I'm telling you to take some risks, to experiment and to stretch yourself. That may make you feel uneasy. Let me share one experience from my schooldays that taught me the value of overcoming that natural reluctance, that fear of failure.

My first real understanding of how being a girl might bring specific challenges came in the sixth form, when at 16 I found myself alone in a class of boys taking Maths at my co-educational state school. We also had two male Maths teachers. Quickly exposed to the difficulties that came with being 'different', I wasn't just left out, but teased mercilessly, particularly when I got anything wrong, which happened often. A vicious circle developed: the more pressure I felt, the less confident and more flustered I became, which only worsened my academic performance. At the end of the first term, I felt miserable and isolated. My parents encouraged me to consider changing subjects. I was reluctant, partly because I could see that my loss in confidence was contributing to the problem. I needed to break the downward spiral.

This class was the 'double maths' group – we were taking Maths and Further Maths A levels. The Further Maths course involved twelve topics. Six were relatively straightforward – but the examiners therefore set quite unpredictable questions that would test real mastery of each subject. Six other topics were deemed hard, but only a narrow set of questions would ever be asked. A candidate had to answer 'just' six questions. A possible way through occurred to me: by mastering the six difficult topics I could predict the questions and be confident that I could answer them.

This may sound an over-ambitious plan for someone towards the bottom of the class, but it worked. I plugged away, one topic at a time, till I conquered six. My new approach and very gradual success (vaguely) impressed the boys and our teachers. Slowly, I became more accepted. Alongside that personal triumph, I could see how the dynamic of that sixth-form Maths class changed. At the start of our two-year course, the group was competitive, and no one helped each other out, even when none of us could solve a problem, but gradually we became more collaborative. We actually started having fun. We also spurred each other on to greater success. It was many years since a pupil from the school had gone to either Oxford or Cambridge University: that year, five of us won places.

One of the results of this episode was that I gained in confidence; but – even more significantly – I learned to find a way through what felt like an impossible situation. This, in fact, is one of the most important tools needed if we are to fulfil our potential in the workplace (and in life generally). Any career is more of a labyrinth than a ladder; there are twists and turns for everyone, man or woman, and dealing with the setbacks, learning how to overcome the natural human reaction of feeling discouraged, of wanting to walk away, is vital. The thing about labyrinths is that if you keep going, even when you seem to be walking back on yourself, you do reach the centre. My daughter Florence and I have walked a labyrinth together several times and every time the experience has a powerful impact, reminding us that we can reach our destination, as long as we persevere.

But we have to stay in the labyrinth to get to the centre. Many years after my sixth-form experience, Lord Davies conducted a survey as part of his Women on Boards review. Over 2,600 people responded – almost 90% of them women. When asked to 'describe any steps you took to overcome particular issues you faced' (in progressing your career) the most frequent response was 'I left the job'. As my own early career experience showed, there may be moments when that is really the only way forward – but it should not be our default option. Things will never change and we will never learn how to overcome obstacles if we always abandon ship. If the cost of childcare, a real problem in the UK in particular, where families spend around a third of their income on nurseries and child-minders, is the issue, discuss that with your boss. I've seen cases where managers simply haven't done the maths – and would actually much rather see what can be done to help than see women leave because it doesn't pay to work. If your career potential is theoretically encouraging but the reality less so, you need to make a judgement – and I would base that on whether the culture is right, whether you have allies who can help you emerge on the other side, or whether you are on your own, in which case it's time to move on.

I have seen many more people regret *not* trying something than trying and falling short. But we do need to deal with the unpredictability of the outcome when we stretch ourselves, to learn to see our shortcomings as just that, rather than fatal blows. I have definitely tested the outer limits of my capabilities, and there have been moments of realisation that I have taken on too much. In March 2013, I was asked by Nick Clegg, then Deputy Prime Minister, to conduct an independent review into the processes and culture within the Liberal Democrats, and to make recommendations for change. The review was prompted by a series of high profile allegations that the Party had failed to act on complaints of sexual harassment made against a former chief executive. I was keen to help if I could and was particularly interested in the focus on culture.

As I gathered evidence for the review, it quickly became clear that the cultural challenges – not just in the Liberal Democrats but in party politics generally – are even more acute than in the corporate sector. Party politics are intrinsically intertwined with the strong forces of personal power and ideology. Intense shared beliefs, coupled with an overt competitiveness in parliamentary politics, create a different situation than in a company. When I was disappointed to be passed over for promotion by my first employer, I was able to leave and find employment elsewhere, at a firm that suited me better. If this early career disappointment had been within the only political party that fitted with my strong ideological beliefs, finding an opportunity elsewhere wouldn't have been an option.

Seeing these issues up close, interviewing people whose whole careers, friendships and in some cases family lives were inextricably tied up with a political party, was an intense experience. The vulnerability of young researchers, interns and volunteers working for powerful politicians was both obvious and disturbing. At the same time, employment practices were often much less formal and protective than in business, as subsequent revelations across Westminster have sadly corroborated. I needed to undertake a comprehensive review, to hear from each and every person who said they had experienced bullying or harassment. At the same time, I couldn't let the review encroach too far on either my job or my family, so I gave myself just six weeks to complete it. This was a Herculean task, and I was on my own, having committed to complete confidentiality for the witnesses. I got up at 3 a.m. each day and worked throughout the weekends. This inevitably took its toll on my health and family life. By the time I emerged, I knew I could not accept such a task again in the context of other big responsibilities.

As we try to encourage the next generation, parents, teachers and mentors need to strike a delicate balance. We do not want girls to be discouraged (especially when their opportunities are greater than ever before) – but neither should we give the impression that everything is solved just yet. I have spoken at many schools; one of the best events was hosted by Wellington College, a private, co-educational school, when Sir Anthony Seldon was an inno-vative and inspiring headmaster. Wellington had invited girls from six other local schools to join their own sixth-form girls at a conference entitled Girls at the Top. What stood out was the candour of the speakers. The message running throughout the day was that the girls had wonderful opportunities ahead but also should be aware that the world is not quite equal. There was no sense of trying to take the wind out of their sails, more of creating awareness, to help them make the right decisions and not fall at the first hurdle if they suffered setbacks. One speaker, a headmistress, also pointed out that while it might feel very distant now, if the girls thought they might want to have children this was something to bear in mind when they were thinking about a career choice. She wasn't discouraging them from aiming for the very top of their chosen field; simply to be mindful of other life ambitions. It's easy to compartmentalise decisions, but they are all connected.

A (male) executive complained to me, 'Young people seem not to just want a job, they want an odyssey.' I thought that it was marvellous to want an epic journey – and I want to encourage you to embark on your own odyssey. Women at all levels have been shown to want work with a purpose beyond earning money and getting promotions. Many of us feel this particularly acutely after having children; after all, the alternative way we might be spending our time is with them, which sets a high bar for fulfilment at work. Now the evidence suggests that as the next generation thinks ahead, both boys and girls want work with 'meaning', employers whose values align with their own, and balance in their lives.

I asked my own children to choose three criteria out of nine that were the most important to them as they thought about their adult lives. All prioritised 'being able to do something that makes a positive difference' and 'having time to spend with my family'. Their third choices were split between 'work–life balance', 'being intellectually or creatively fulfilled' and 'achieving my full potential'. No one chose 'making a lot of money' or 'getting to the top' as one of their top three goals.

My children's answers are very similar to those given by a group of nearly 21,000 university students as part of a 30% Club study conducted over 2015 and 2016. Much of the commentary on this generation focuses on their problems – insecurities and pressures relating to social media, along with economic uncertainties compared with previous generations as they enter the workforce, including significant student debt. These are real challenges but far from the whole story.

In 2014, a young Modern Languages undergraduate at Cambridge University, Helena Eccles, approached me with the idea of exploring how today's students might view their own career prospects. Ambitious and clever, Helena had been surprised by what she quickly recognised to be career barriers for women during a gap year working for a well-established, traditional firm (this may sound familiar). My younger namesake suspected that our efforts to encourage women in the workplace might be too late even by the time graduates start their careers – that their choices and ambitions may already have been influenced by their early workplace experiences along with perceptions formed through the media and other sources.

The 30% Club embarked on a pilot study at Cambridge University. Over 1,000 undergraduates, 42% of them male, completed an extensive survey about what they wanted out of life and a career, and their perceptions of the opportunities ahead. We wanted to explore both what young men and women had in common as they looked ahead, and also where their views about career prospects might differ.

Work–life balance (a term that had not even been coined when I was a student) scored over 90% as a high priority issue. It's worth pointing out that this survey was not conducted in the street or by phone, where students might have felt pressured to prioritise 'nice' ambitions – they completed it in their own time and rooms.

There was just one big difference in views between male and female students at Cambridge. Over half the women said they would be hesitant about applying for male-dominated sectors such as financial services or management consultancy because they thought this would limit their career prospects. Only 18% of men said they would be hesitant about entering 'female-dominated' sectors (education, retail).

Of course, Cambridge University is not necessarily representative of the broader student population, so we extended the study. Twenty-one universities across the UK and Ireland took part, with over 20,000 student respondents covering a wide range of socio-economic backgrounds and degree disciplines. We also extended the pilot questions to explore some areas in more depth.

As we saw at Cambridge, a high proportion (55%) of female students across the broader population said that a sector's 'male-dominated' reputation would make them hesitant to apply. As we expanded the question set we learned that young women feel confident in their abilities but even before they start work, they are not convinced that they will be able to progress, in any sector. Only 42% of female students felt confident that their gender would have no bearing on their career progression or pay, compared with 72% of men. This compares closely with surveys of women and men actually in work: less than half the female respondents to Project 28–40 were confident that women and men at the same level earned the same in their organisation, compared with three-quarters of male respondents. There is a gender *perception* gap, as well as a gender *pay* gap.

The 30% Club's student study confirmed that almost all (93%) of the young men and women at university today are looking for a career that 'makes a difference'. This is a huge and welcome shift from the past, when my generation expected less of an odyssey and was very focused on making money for ourselves. I believe that today we don't need to *choose* between profit and purpose – commercially successful businesses over the long term will be the ones with strong values. Smart companies get this and are looking to align with the next generation's values.

At a time of considerable change and uncertainty, young people may be understandably worried about their future, but should also be aware of their own power. In addition to all the other good things about them, having strong values is now seen as important. Digital expertise is also highly sought after: those who've grown up with technology can help businesses understand new behaviours. Again, difference really can be an advantage – and you should 'work it'.

The most important thing is not to let any preconceptions put you off from doing what you really want to do, or in any way dent your ambitions and expectations. We can choose to reject the perceived limitations, but we have to get our mind around them, to see that we can succeed. It is not inevitable that you will be hard done by – in fact, with all the emphasis on gender balance, there's plenty of reason to be cheerful, and to aim high.

That's not the starting point for many young women today. During my talks (often to all-girl groups) at schools, universities, business schools and to early-career women, the same questions come up time and again. Here is the most frequently asked 'top ten'.

Girls' Frequently Asked Questions

1. Do you feel people make assumptions about you because you are a woman? What do you do when that happens?

2. Is having children still seen as a problem? How long should you take as maternity leave? Is it a bad idea to work flexibly?

3. How do you achieve work–life balance? Is it all down to your husband?

4. Do you worry about failing?

5. How do I get started in my career if I don't know the right people or I'm not even sure what I want to do?

6. Do you think it's hard to make progress in a male-dominated industry? (Or sometimes, the opposite question, 'Do you think that sometimes you've just been given opportunities because you are a woman?') What do you do if someone is patronising towards you?

7. How can you tell what a company's culture is like before you join? What do you do if you experience sexual harassment or discrimination?

8. Is it important to have a mentor? Did you have one? Do you have one?

9. Have you found women often don't support other women?

10. Do you think men need to change as well as women?

When we read this whole set of questions we see an under-current of anxiety running through them. They do not add up to 'I'm great, tell me how I can get on'. And they most certainly do not suggest girls feel they 'own the process'. The skew is 'Please tell me how not to fail within the exist-ing set-up' rather than 'Please tell me how to create my own conditions for success'. It's an important distinction – we behave differently if we are trying to avoid mistakes than if we are going for gold. The questions reflect where girls are today, more anxious than excited. They are genu-inely concerned, so of course I try to address what's actu-ally on their minds, not what I wish they were asking:

1. *Do you feel people make assumptions about you because are a woman? What do you do when that happens?*
Yes – though much less now than thirty years ago.
People tend to project their own expectations onto others – which obviously tells us more about them than anything else. It's been assumed, for example, that as a 'working mother' I may not want to take on a new role, even where it might have been something I really wanted (and was able) to do.
There's just been no discussion about it at all, apart from after the fact when I've tried not to fall in line with their inaccurate image of me, but to clearly and calmly set the record straight. I try to engage rather than to push back, to encourage the other person to see me in a different light – and then I've

found they actually do. And I try not to take it personally: behaviours are learned throughout life and although your boss might consider himself to be very attuned to diverse talent, he may need to 'undo' years of conventional thinking. Help him out.

2. Is having children still seen as a problem? How long should you take as maternity leave? Flexible working?

It would be naïve to assume no one flinches when a valued member of their team announces they are pregnant – even if that's just because they will be missed while they are away. But you can pre-empt any assumptions being made about your future plans by speaking up, telling your manager that you remain ambitious, including if you are also requesting a change in your hours. Employers can't ask about your intentions but you can tell them. If you change your mind, that is fine. But never leave a void to be filled. Two of my colleagues handled it perfectly; they each came to see me and both made it clear that their impending motherhood did not change their commitment (although they expressed this in a very human way), both lobbied for interesting new challenges right up to when they went on maternity leave, they used 'keep in touch' days while on leave and continued to progress after they returned, irrespective of working flexibly. Their partners also took shared parental leave. It all seemed very modern and very natural. There is no right or wrong amount of maternity leave – it's a very personal thing, but I urge you not to let fear get in the way of what seems right for you and your family. Just keep talking to your employer as your plans evolve.

3. How do you achieve work–life balance?
Balance means different things to different people. In many ways, I'm still working on this – because I adore my family and also love what I do. My mother tells me I have always taken the 'hard road' but it would be more accurate to say I have not chosen the easy one. It would have been easier not to have had so many children, for example, but much less fun, exciting and joyful. There are strange moments: I find myself putting on washing machine loads covering the individual colours of the rainbow rather than just dark or light (yes, I have done orange washes). Packing for holidays (eleven pairs of flip-flops) is another logistical challenge – but a small price to pay. It's important to think of work as part of your life, not separate from life – not least because we spend so much time working.

Technology has been a great enabler. At the beginning of my career, there was no internet, no mobile phones, and the limitations on staying in touch outside the office were very restrictive. Now, of course, we may struggle to switch off, but in theory we have much more flexibility. In practice, many businesses still have a culture of presenteeism – the pressure to come to the office, to sit at your desk. We need to keep demonstrating that we can do a great job wherever we are, that it's our output that matters. I have become more confident about that, but know we still have to keep showing that agile working helps make us most productive.

Secondly, we need to be clear about what really matters to us and make that sacrosanct. For my family, it's been important that I get home most nights in time for family supper. If we have two, or sometime three (because of travel) evenings without that time, the dynamic shifts, we all feel a bit destabilised, I feel unhappy, the children get stressed and even the amazingly patient Richard gets worn down.

4. Do you worry about failing?

I am completely normal so yes, the fear of failure is there, but I have also learned to recognise that every day is full of triumphs and disasters and, as Rudyard Kipling said in his wonderful poem 'If', we need to 'treat those two impostors just the same'. I do and will fail. It may seem a frivolous example, but I recently made a pavlova (well, I tried) for an extended family lunch. Usually, this is one of the very few dishes I can easily make, with or without help from my daughters. On this occasion, it took three attempts and 24 eggs (we had a lot of scrambled eggs using the yolks that week) to make even a passable meringue, and even then it needed restyling as 'Eton mess' (the pavlova is crushed and mixed with strawberries and cream). After the first two flops, I completely overreacted: the failed meringues became a motif for all the things I felt I was getting wrong in my life. As Richard told me, it was a reminder of the importance of coping with failure, whether big or small.

5. How do I get started in my career if I don't know the right people or I'm not even sure what I want to do?
You need practical help. Do not be afraid of asking. Even if you, your friends and family know absolutely nobody in the field you are interested in, it is possible to create leads. Write to people. In particular, showcase any difference. If you are the first person in your family to go to university, make that clear, make it an advantage, not an obstacle. See if your school can get someone in the industry along to speak – in the UK there are great organisations like Speakers for Schools that can help. I have spoken at schools where young people have written to me afterwards, very specifically requesting my help, and I always like the way they take the initiative. If I can help, I will. The

apprenticeship schemes offered by many companies and industries are another way of getting that first break. We all need someone to take a chance on us early on – the key is to demonstrate that you might have something they may not already have.

6. Do you think it's harder making progress in a male-dominated industry? (Or the opposite?) What do you do if someone is patronising towards you?
As my own experience suggests, this really can cut both ways. It can be lonely and it's easy to feel excluded (even if this is in no way intended by your colleagues), but you can also be noticed more easily. I would not discourage anyone from following their dream if it happens to be in an industry that is male-dominated. Just be aware, do not take it for granted that your skills and efforts will be recognised, and seek to make a deliberate impact. Whatever you do, do not just try to 'be like the boys'.

If you experience patronising behaviour then point it out, not aggressively (at least not at first) or emotionally, but calmly, giving the protagonist an opportunity to apologise or explain. If that isn't forthcoming, or the behaviour persists, talk to someone you trust, one of your allies or a colleague in HR. Don't feel resentful or powerless.

I am concerned about positive discrimination. A brilliant man should not be overlooked in favour of a less talented woman, and if that's being considered it means that business leaders (or other selectors) aren't really thinking about what we are trying to achieve through encouraging diversity. Excluding people just because of their gender, race or sexual orientation, if they are male, white and straight, takes us right back to where we started. Ultimately, the emphasis on a person's 'identity' should lessen, but for now we do need to call people out if they are biasing selection against talent of the 'wrong' sort. It makes no sense to try to solve one form of injustice by applying another.

7. How can you tell what a company's culture is like in advance? What do you do if you experience sexual harassment or discrimination?
Trying to accurately gauge a company's culture from the outside is tricky – you are looking for clues and corroboration. Ask as many people as you can – ideally including recent joiners as well as your interviewers – and read widely, to see what's said about the company (I am sceptical, however, about anonymous reviews). Quite simply, ask 'How would you describe the culture?' If the words used are broadly consistent from one future colleague to the next, it is an encouraging sign that what they are saying is really lived and breathed. If the answers fit in with what's valuable to you, go for it. There may well be individuals who are 'rogue' within the firm, but if the core is strong, that will prevail.

If it turns out that the reality is quite different, then my general advice is to learn quickly and move on. But if you experience genuine sex discrimination – such as becoming aware you are being paid less than a man doing the same job – or harassment, please speak up rather than just leave. You have a voice, and these days it will be heard. By coming forward, you can improve the situation for both yourself and others.

How you escalate a problem is important, though. The #MeToo campaign that followed after the Harvey Weinstein scandal broke may have dramatically made the point that sexual harassment goes way beyond one man, industry or country, but tweeting about your specific problem at work is unlikely to be the best way of resolving it. You need to act as quickly as you can after an incident, and you must follow procedures. Usually that means reporting the issue to your manager (unless they are the perpetrator) or Human Resources, who are required to carry out an unbiased investigation. This can be an uncomfortable process but if your complaint is justified, employment law will protect you. No decent (or even merely up-to-date) organisation will sweep the matter under the carpet – especially after all the adverse publicity around badly-handled cases. If you feel no one is taking you seriously, make a formal written complaint using your employer's grievance procedures. If this still doesn't work, the next step is to go to employment tribunal. That may sound very daunting: free advice is available online and the very act of starting the process may result in a successful resolution.

I am quite often asked if bringing a case to tribunal will affect future employability. Again, if it is justified and the claims are proportionate, it should not. Over a decade ago, a senior female executive sued the investment bank where she worked for £7.5 million, alleging sex discrimination and unequal pay. The extraordinarily high sum of damages sought, especially relative to the allegations, did not help her case (she lost) – or the reputation of women in the City. One of the pivotal incidences involved her being asked to pour drinks for male colleagues on a flight on the company's jet. The tribunal found that she happened to be seated nearest the drinks cabinet and that anyone who had sat there would have been asked to do the same. It's important to retain perspective. (After that particular lawsuit, whenever I went to pour the coffee in a meeting, the men present would rush up and take over.)

8. *Is it important to have a mentor? Did you have one? Do you have one?*
As we've seen, it is really important to have allies and advisers. They do not need to be formal mentors. Stewart Newton was de facto my early

mentor, but we did not have a formal mentoring relationship. Look for at least one person who is senior to you, whom you trust, who has your best interests at heart and whose opinion you value. I still have people I turn to, Sir Roger Carr, for example, who has always been very thoughtful and generous with his time. He and a couple of others have effectively mentored me through times of change in particular. Ultimately, you are leading your own life, but it is really important to have sounding boards and that reality-check mirror.

9. Have you found that women don't support other women?

Nowadays, I see little evidence of the Queen Bee syndrome, where one woman wants all the attention. I've personally benefited from female mentors – the late Dame Helen Alexander, former chief executive of The Economist Group, was described by its eponymous publication as relying on a 'quiet wisdom: listening not lecturing' and I can vouch for that. While I was 'between jobs' after Newton, Helen offered to meet and after listening carefully to various ideas I was exploring, gave me the clearest-sighted advice. She was adamant about where my strengths lay, and quite determined that I should not 'settle' for anything that didn't really play to those strengths. She helped me make up my mind about my future – and I will always be grateful to Helen for being so genuine in her desire to help.

The data confirms that women who are successful in business do tend to look out for their female colleagues. Credit Suisse Research Institute's Gender 3000 report is unambiguous: 'female CEOs are 50% more likely to have a female Chief Finance Officer and 55% more likely to have women running business units'.

The *perception* that 'women don't look out for other women' may emanate from the reluctance of some senior women to get involved in anything that looks like a campaign. I have seen that and think it's a shame but understandable based on past perceptions of gender equality being regarded as a 'women's issue', not a business issue. Some of these women have become more involved as the agenda has shifted; others have admitted that they thought progress would occur naturally. Dame Marjorie Scardino, the first female chief executive of a FTSE-100 company, said when she stood down in 2012 after fifteen years, 'I thought … that by the time I left Pearson things would be different in terms of how many women there were as chief executives or chairmen or board members. It's not too different and for that I'm sorry.' Dame Marjorie revealed, 'I have always thought it was not helpful to just pile women on to boards because they were women.' I hope by now it's clear that the 30% Club never had any intention of doing that.

10. Do you think men need to change as well as women?

Few of the men I know of my age (or older) would have been prepared to do what my husband has done, but I think that is related to expectations they grew up with about their role. As we have seen, this is changing: young men today expect to have a different, more balanced life. I've been challenged about this; it's suggested that these young men are idealistic and when they start work, they will quickly fall into line with past behaviours, but I am more confident. Already, men are much less proud of working long hours – that now seems less a badge of honour and more a sign of not being in control of their own destiny. The cool, really successful men work the hours they choose and have plenty of time for other activities. I am writing this after talking to a colleague who works extended hours for four days to spend Tuesdays with his three-and-a-half-year-old daughter. It's Monday today, and he has been talking about the day ahead with great enthusiasm, describing it as a highlight of his week.

But while things are changing for men, again as with women, we're not there yet. The UK government introduced Shared Parental Leave in April 2015. Just 3,000 couples took shared leave in the first three months of 2016 compared with 155,000 mothers taking old-style maternity leave (and 52,000 fathers on shorter paternity leave). In 2018, the take-up of shared parental leave was still only around 2% of eligible couples. However, companies have tended to offer men and women different financial treatment if they share parental leave, leaving most couples worse off than if the mother takes all the leave. A few firms have taken the trail-blazing decision to treat all new parents equally (and however they come to be parents); they have been rewarded by an immediate positive reaction from both staff and media that will hopefully encourage others to follow suit. I am convinced that many men want to play an active role in their children's lives and I'd love to see 'high flyers' blaze that trail and show that taking parental leave for a few months is entirely consistent with having a great, multi-decade career. After all, why not?

I am always happy to try to answer whatever is on girls' minds – but the one question I really want to hear, that rarely comes up is, quite simply:

'How do I get to be the CEO?'

Chapter 8

Camp CEO

Girlguiding research has found that 90% of 9 to 10 year olds think that women and men have the same chance at succeeding in their jobs – but only 35% of 17 to 21 year olds feel the same. Camp CEO is about changing that.

WWW.GIRLGUIDING.ORG.UK

In 2014, I was invited to speak at the UK Girl Guides' 'Camp CEO'. There I met some amazingly ambitious and impressive 14–17-year-old girls, who had been through a rigorous application process to be picked for a week-long intensive course that included mentoring, challenges and talks from female CEOs. I loved the concept – and not just because I enjoyed my time as a rather manic Brownie, when I drove my parents mad in my quest to break the regional record for the most badges. The very idea of a CEO boot camp reminded me that far too often, efforts to help women progress focus on everything *except* preparing them for that top job.

Much of the advice doled out to women of all ages focuses on self-improvement. It's fine to be encouraged to be the best version of ourselves but not to feel we have to change radically or that we must walk along a narrow tightrope to succeed. Such advice erodes rather than builds our confidence: it's so easy to become focused on what we are doing 'wrong' rather than what we are getting right.

Sylvia Ann Hewlett has conducted ground-breaking research into a wide range of aspects of diversity, including gender. Her book *Executive Presence* explores the missing link between women's merit and their success. Sylvia suggests that female leaders have little latitude and she describes the thin line women have to tread so as not to appear 'too aggressive/not assertive enough', 'too opinionated or shrill/unable to command a room', 'too provocatively dressed/too frumpy', 'looking too young/looking too old'. The barrage of dos and don'ts is exhausting. If we worried too much about these 'female appearance blunders' we might never get out of bed. Happily, having shown us what can go wrong, Sylvia concludes that simply looking polished and groomed is actually the most important appearance criterion for would-be female executives.

It is time we women stopped worrying about being 'too this' or 'too that' and instead focused much more on getting the job we want. (Let's assume a reasonable level of ability, qualifications and an aptitude for hard work.

No career advice can substitute for those attributes.) One of the first steps is to celebrate what we do well and spend more time on the areas of our life that we enjoy. I include myself in that. There are a few things we can consciously do to help ourselves be happier and more accomplished in our own eyes.

First, try (really hard) not to look over your shoulder and compare yourself with anyone else. Looking sideways gets us nowhere – and contentment is an absolute, not a relative state. Focus on understanding what works for you, including when you are at your most energetic and effective. Newspaper articles often make a point of refer- encing how early I and some other 'successful' women get up in the morning as if that's part of a plan – but what they don't mention is that I have always been an early riser – and early to bed. I cannot function intellectually past 9 p.m., and I do my best work in the mornings. Getting up early is part of my natural rhythm (and annoys my family at the weekends), not a 'beating the competition' strategy.

A quick look through what's been written about me also reveals more than a few comments about my style of dress, often conveying surprise that I don't 'look like' a senior City woman – or a mother of nine (whatever she is supposed to look like). I do like pink and I do like dresses, but before you picture me as a (much) older version of Elle Woods, Reese Witherspoon's fabulous character in *Legally Blonde*, I'm afraid the reality is much less exciting. The only statement I am making in my choice of clothes is that we can be *feminine without being frivolous*. I do feel more powerful in my work dresses, colourful though they may be, and as we explored earlier, feeling that way means that I am in turn perceived as being more powerful. I took many years to reach that point, and needed to escape my own 'crazy mirror' when it came to my appearance. That mirror became especially warped in my teenage years; I was anorexic between the ages of fourteen and fifteen. The distortions in my mind's eye were so acute that I thought I was 'fat' when I weighed five stone (32 kg). Now I can see my body more objectively – a long way from perfect, but quite lean and strong – after all, it has managed to produce all those children – and I know what suits me. My 'look' involves simple dresses (often cut or coloured quirkily), unfussy but bold jewellery and high heels that lift me up, both literally and psychologically. I rarely wear suits: structured clothes feel like barriers between me and the world. That may sound odd, but I just don't feel comfortable on days when I 'have to' wear a suit. So much for strong-shouldered power dressing.

In the early days of my career when money for clothes was scarce, my wardrobe was very limited, especially since the high street wasn't as great as it is now. These days I enjoy getting ready, although in fact it takes just a few minutes from top to toe – and then getting on with the real business of living. My simple formula is certainly not for everyone; one stylish friend, lawyer Tamara Box, has a different-coloured pair of glasses to match every outfit; another, Sian Westerman, an investment banker involved in the British Fashion Council, is wonderfully cutting-edge. Dame Inga Beale, doyenne of the insurance industry, dresses very confidently, with particularly striking jewellery. FTSE-100 CEO Dame Carolyn McCall is a non-executive director at Burberry and often wears their great clothes. I love seeing what these powerful women are wearing but their distinctive looks don't influence my own style.

In areas of both style and substance, the key is to develop your own view, a strong inner compass to guide you in most situations and decisions, big and small. I once took part in a conference on economics and politics alongside Lord Forsyth, former Secretary of State for Scotland, who explained that in Margaret Thatcher's government, long before the days of WhatsApp, texts or even emails, ministers didn't need to be told how to respond to an unexpected development; the central view was strong enough for them to be able to react 'on message'. As individuals, we need a similarly strong core, as the saying goes, 'if you don't believe in anything, you'll fall for everything'.

But much of the guidance given to women doesn't help us become more centred. Ironically, it's usually based on teaching us how to play the (past) men's game, just as men move on from that. Women in mid-career are bombarded with advice on how to network, how to be more assertive, how to dress for success. While we are doing all that, men are taking aim at the role they want. We are embarking on a much more convoluted route, sometimes without even knowing where we are going – so it's hardly surprising that we are more likely to get lost along the way. There couldn't be a better time to take a more direct approach: having made some progress in the boardroom, the emphasis now is on encouraging the appointment of more women executives. It's not just a good time to be a girl, it's a wonderful time to be an ambitious woman. If you want to be the CEO, or even just to progress to the next level, concentrate on 'getting on the bench', not on joining yet another women's network.

But what does getting on the bench entail? I am a big believer in clarifying things (or establishing what's not clear) by writing them down. List the attributes of the role – does it involve managing a team? Presenting to clients? Devising a business plan? – and then consider which skills you already have and the ones you may be missing. Notoriously, women will list few skills and lots of gaps, so if you can't be fair to yourself, seek someone else's opinion. Then think about how to address any *vital* gaps – but don't even *think* about needing to close them all. Executive search consultants confirm what sounds like an exaggeration, that a woman may fulfil eight out of ten requirements for a job but think she's not up to it, whereas a man might have five and believe it's rightfully his.

Alongside this self-assessment, work out a plan to *position* yourself for the role in the eyes of those who will be making the decision. Do you have good exposure to them? Do they get to see what you can do? Might they have misconceptions about you? You need them to be thinking about you quite specifically as a strong candidate for the job you want, not just in a vaguely positive light. You should signal your ambition overtly – people will think carefully about turning you down if you have made it clear that you want the role. It may be unfair, but those who take disappointments meekly are more likely to be disappointed. And, most importantly of all, think about how you come across; do you behave as if you are a leader, part of the future management team? Are you proactive with your ideas, do you speak up, encourage your colleagues and operate as if you merit the next job? I have participated in many succession-planning conversations, where senior managers are considering who to 'put on the bench' for their own role and their direct reports. The difference between those assessed as top talent and those who are simply regarded as capable usually comes down to *how they conduct themselves*.

Don't worry that any of this sounds pushy. Studies like the 30% Club's *Cracking the Code* confirm that women tend to express our ambition *ambiguously*, and that gives very mixed signals to bosses looking for clues. Help them out here. This is not about 'acting like a man', it's about acting like someone preparing for the next role. So often, I've seen women being overlooked because it's assumed that they are not particularly interested – yet they have been waiting politely for someone to ask.

And don't think you need to clone someone one step ahead of you, to catch them up. Remember, there is a widespread understanding in business today that there are different ways of being effective; being authentic is valuable. Your own natural abilities are the ones to develop, not someone else's. Good bosses love discovering great talent, it helps them and the whole business – and that's strong motivation for them to help you succeed.

These suggestions demand a degree of optimism on your part. If we're optimistic, we expect to win (even games of chance) and we take risks, putting ourselves out there. What about the many women who feel disillusioned or dispirited as a result of the not-yet-equal workplace? The picture portrayed by surveys like Project 28–40, or frankly by any group of mid-career women talking about their career experiences, is a sobering one. Discouraging workplaces take their toll. And women who stopped working to focus on their young families or elderly relatives feel a different frustration; they may be keen to resume a career but unsure if that's even possible or how to take the first step. Life blows such as divorce, illness or separation may also have intervened, causing financial anxiety as well as emotional trauma. A quick glance at the pages in newspapers targeted at female readers suggests that more of us feel anxious than fulfilled in our forties and fifties.

If you are in this situation, the first goal is to break the negative spiral. I know that is (much) easier said than done. It is hard to pick ourselves up when we feel worn down. We need something good to happen to break the negative cycle and that does not always occur at the moment we really need it. I have been very fortunate in my life but still found it disconcerting when I stepped down as Newton's CEO. I had been at the company for such a long time and had really 'grown up' (and older) with my colleagues. It was quite hard to look ahead and there were many days when I struggled to take my own advice. I knew I needed mental space, to carefully consider the next phase – and I also needed to replenish my energy and enthusiasms. During this time of uncertainty, when my future was a blank page, I worried I would diminish, not grow. It was one of those punctuation points in life: how could I build on what I had learned?

Those who've been through truly extreme life experiences have much to teach us. During this time of introspection – and quite by chance – I met a woman whose inner confidence shone brightly; after we had been talking for a while, she told me that a decade earlier she had been diagnosed with Stage 4 breast cancer and been given a very slim chance of survival. Now, every moment, every birthday was a bonus and she wasted no time at all, appreciating it as a precious gift. Our conversation quickly moved beyond the usual superficial small talk between people meeting for the first time. We talk in clichés of 'putting things in perspective' when we hear about such experiences, but this stranger really did help me to think more clearly. I was wrestling with many feelings – and practicalities – but they would all be much more likely to fall into place if I followed my inner compass, if I stayed true to my own principles. If I was open to possibilities, those possibilities would be more likely to arise. I also really wanted to enjoy the time with my family while I was at home. Walking my youngest daughter to school each day, having more leisurely conversations, catching up with friends – and savouring each birthday (there were six family birthdays during my four months' break). As we enjoyed yet another cake the other day we counted up the children's aggregate birthdays since Fitz was born – we are up to 154. That really is something to marvel at.

The school attended by three of my daughters has a beautifully named 'enrichment programme'. This time of reflection was part of my enrichment, but what about the very practical issues of finding another job? Here my advice is simple: even if you are relatively senior, do not rely on executive search firms to find you that next wonderful role. It may happen – but in my experience this would be a stroke of luck rather than a reliable plan. I was clear that, aged fifty, I wanted another executive, full-time role; not the same type of management position I had just left but to *build* something. Perhaps in another decade or so, I might be interested in non-executive roles. Many women tell me – and I am sure the same is true for men – that they struggle to get meetings with the leading search firms. I knew many search consultants well, partly through their involvement with the 30% Club, and was encouraged that they were receptive. During our meetings, I outlined my clear goals. Over the next few months I was shown a number of *non-executive* board roles, big charity jobs or opportunities to chair companies going through a private equity buyout. Several consultants were very enthusiastic but I was not shown one single 'hands-on' *executive* position by any of them. At the same time, a few people I knew who were involved in interesting ventures contacted me, and in some cases I contacted them. Several offered me executive positions, including of course the role I was delighted to accept at Legal and General Investment Management (LGIM), where my (big) ambition is to engage the nation in investing, to reach those who haven't invested before – particularly women and younger people. That really excites me; the role combines 'building something' with trying to help people improve their financial health. Exactly what I wanted: an executive role that combines profit and purpose. But the *process* of finding what turned out to be a dream job was quite different to my expectations at the start. It was easy to talk to people I had worked with in various contexts and everyone I contacted directly was very generous with their time, advice and, in some cases, offers. As we find with so much of the conventional career toolkit, formal processes don't necessarily help us in reality – but those allies and mentors we have talked about really can. It's all about relationships, and it's important to prioritise building those over time. A sponsor – someone who goes further, who champions your career – is ideal, but usually only available to those who've already proven themselves, as the sponsor is putting their own credibility on the line. Remember, take it one step at a time, and the path will gradually open up.

When I joined LGIM, several young women proactively reached out to tell me how happy they were that I had joined the company. One email in particular summed up the universality of the challenges of working motherhood:

> I read your article in the Evening Standard titled: 'Working Women: Get a seat at the table and change the culture'. It was one of my best reads as yet because your story resonated with me, and the strength and understanding showed in your marriage meant a lot to me as a married mother of two. I started to think if she can do it, then I can. So, thank you for inspiring me.
>
> At the time, I had applied to do my MBA which I did and finished last year. I even told everyone I knew about you – how you juggled a big family with working as a CEO of an asset manager. For me, from that day onward, I stopped being hard on myself – forever feeling guilty that I wasn't spending as much time with the kids – which of course, hindered my ability to want to aim higher, as I felt more responsibility = less flexibility which would mean spending even less time with the family. In a nutshell, reading your article was a call to me to say, *it's OK to aim high, find the right balance and everyone will be fine*. [her emphasis] So, thank you very much.

Let's talk about this big sense of conflict. Many women are not just worried about the impact having children will have on their career but about the impact their career might have on their children.

More than two-thirds of the female respondents to Project 28–40 said they felt society expected them to prioritise family over work. In my view this is only partly attributable to media pressure; the pressure also emanates from ourselves.

Both attitudes and working practices have moved on a long way since I had Fitz in 1991 but the reality is that having children is not something to fit neatly into a busy life. It's complicated, emotionally and physically, and changes us – often in very good ways. Again, there are as many lives as there are people, as many childbearing experiences as there are mothers, but we share common strands of experience.

Although Richard and I (obviously) had no fertility issues, I did not have straightforward pregnancies. My first pregnancy was especially difficult: I was underweight to start with, barely 46 kg, but lost rather than gained weight over the first four months, through acute 'morning' sickness (mine lasted all day). Travelling into work was hard: I had to take a bus then the Underground, but couldn't make the train journey in one go, so allowed enough time to come up to be sick, once if not twice during the journey. It was a tough time physically: apart from a threatened miscarriage at fourteen weeks, when I had to spend two weeks in bed, I kept working the same long hours throughout until diagnosed with pre-eclampsia (a condition where the mother's blood pressure rises to a dangerous level) and having the baby early.

As I struggled through that first pregnancy, there was one other woman I could compare notes with at work: she was ten years older than me and also expecting her first child. The company employed several hundred staff in London at the time: she was one of only two senior women and I was in awe of her. Our coincidental pregnancies created a bonding experience: we were both nervous first-time mothers and towards the end of the day she would often come up to my desk from the floor where she worked and we would discuss things like whether drinking coffee might affect the baby (neither of us had any clue and there was no search engine to help at the time). After both of us left the firm, our paths crossed several times, and at some point in our conversations we usually talked about our firstborns. As by far the junior person in that relationship, I really welcomed her reaching out to me. Much later, at Newton, we introduced an optional 'buddy' programme to help expectant mothers, where they could choose to have a mentor who had been through the maternity leave experience and returned to work.

The first stages of pregnancy can be a lonely time for women, with most of us wanting to have the 12-week scan before we tell anyone beyond our immediate family, yet often feeling at our worst during the first trimester. I talked about this with a young American woman I know well, who I had seen in New York when she was around two and a half months pregnant, expecting her first child. I had guessed: there is something very telltale about how our bodies change, but I hadn't said anything, although I was longing to congratulate her. When we spoke on the phone a couple of weeks later and she started by telling me her news I mentioned that I had thought so, and she then explained how awful she had been feeling, how she had tried to not let any evidence of the pregnancy show, how she had dealt with the pressures of that particular day, when she had to give a speech. Her struggle was very familiar to me.

We are also used to hearing sad tales of women who have suffered multiple miscarriages, but beyond their relationship are alone with their sorrow. I have had two: one very early, the other at twelve weeks, and found the loneliness of my sadness very hard, especially trying to carry on at work – even, on one occasion, actually having the miscarriage in the office – as if nothing was happening.

My adverse experiences may put you off – please don't let them. It's important that we don't airbrush reality. Much is written about 'unobtainable' role models and I have been cited many times in such articles. I flicked through my youngest daughter's Religious Studies coursework the other day and was intrigued to find a worksheet entitled 'Jesus as a role model'. I felt that rather settled it, that we need a new concept, focused on inspiring without the pressure to emulate. I want to share the reality and encourage you to recognise that everyone has challenges;

the key is to have a supportive environment and to be resilient or adaptable but not aim to be superhuman.

It's wonderful that celebrities like Serena Williams and Beyoncé have opened up about their struggles around maternity, in Serena Williams' case, feeling she 'was not a good mom', while Beyoncé has shared her medical traumas ahead of the birth of her twins by emergency Caesarean, and how she came to accept the way her body has changed. By sharing these experiences they have used their power to reassure other mothers about the commonality of many of our challenges.

And the guilt thing specifically ... where to start? I have not overcome this, but it would surely make me less human if I did. It would be odd not to want to spend time with my children, not to miss them when I'm away, not to feel sad if they are upset when I am leaving the house. Karen Peetz, formerly President of BNY Mellon and the mother of now-grown-up twins, offered some pragmatism at an event hosted by Lloyds Bank. She recognised the need to accept the decisions she had made, the path she was actually taking, rather than to keep wondering about other versions of her life. That enabled her to focus on her career while doing her best when she was at home, enjoying that family time rather than regretting there wasn't more of it. Otherwise, we can end up feeling like we are failing wherever we are – and that is most definitely a recipe for unhappiness.

One of the strangely reassuring aspects of having so many children is that even if I was at home, there wouldn't be enough parents to go around. The dynamic of a large family is inevitably quite different from a smaller one. There is an inbuilt network, for a start. I love seeing the older children spontaneously help their siblings, with their homework, with their friendship issues, with creative projects. (As I am writing this, two of the girls are in the room next door, and I can hear the 17-year-old patiently explaining long multiplication to her 10-year-old sister who struggles with maths. What's especially lovely is that I know the older girl has a lot of her own work to do, but is acting as if she has all the time in the world.) They are perfectly normal children and so there are plenty of scraps, but they are first and foremost a unit.

Meanwhile Richard and I have just been making the best of it. And sometimes we have to see the funny side of the many challenges.

In common with many families, it is not at all unusual in our household to have a completely unanticipated task thrown at us early in the day. One morning two of the children announced over breakfast that they needed to go to school that day in Mexican dress and a Peter Pan costume, respectively. After mentioning as casually as I could that next time it might be useful to know in advance, I tried to think calmly. There was no point panicking, no point stressing our already rather chaotic morning further by complaining – and in the scheme of things, this was not exactly a major problem. I asked if anyone had any ideas. One child remembered a big straw hat that could work as a sombrero, another rummaged around and found a multicoloured poncho and I located a brightly coloured cotton tiered skirt. Luckily our 'Mexican for the day' has long, almost black hair so that helped give the 'look' some authenticity. (As I've mentioned before, luck plays a part.) The Peter Pan costume was more challenging, but as we talked about what we could use, we remembered a green hat with a feather that had been used for a Robin Hood outfit, unearthed some green tights and then did our best to adapt a Christmas Elf tunic. Not a prize-winning outfit but good enough (and then we all had a good laugh about our reality-TV-esque early morning challenge). When Richard and I had just a few children, I loved making special dressing-up clothes for them, efforts that were definitely labours of love rather than because I had any talent. Letting go of the perfectionist trait, just doing what we can, helps us to stretch to fit the tasks in front of us and to be less stressed. For much the same reason, I only write out our family schedule board one day at a time – a week or a month ahead would feel too overwhelming, with all the variables and contingencies. That doesn't mean we don't plan things like holidays (it is important to book ahead if your group numbers 11 – or 14 now that the eldest three have partners), or the vague outline of the next few weekends, but we do try to live in the moment and enjoy the present.

It's obvious, but we can have a lot more valuable mental space if we don't waste energy on negative thoughts, or agonise over everything. When I feel anxious, I frequently turn to someone else, usually my husband, but sometimes a colleague, friend or one of the children (I have noticed they love to help). Even if the subject is not really something they know much about, a kind word or a hug can help everything seem less onerous and put whatever we are wrestling with in perspective.

There's one piece of advice I came across very recently that encapsulates what has made the difference for me between having a 'successful' business career in the eyes of others and actually feeling happy and confident that I am making a valuable contribution outside as well as inside the home. Indian Hindu monk Swami Vivekananda (1863–1902) said, 'Take up one idea. Make that one idea your life, think of it, dream of it, live on that idea. Let the brain, muscles, nerves, every part of your body, be full of that idea and just leave every other idea alone. This is the way to success.' My 'idea' is the big rebalance between men and women – something that has ramifications for my family life, for my roles in business, for the commentary and analysis and speeches I make – and yes, is the motivation behind this book. All roads lead back to this idea. It's obviously far from a new idea, but it often feels to me that people don't understand how powerful a genuine balancing would be and my contribution is to try to change that.

This is my perspective, perhaps my justification – what do my children think? I asked them for their views on being brought up in a family where the traditional parental roles have been reversed. A number of the children suggested that the experience of having many siblings, both brothers and sisters, had also influenced their thinking about gender. We talked, too, about whether they felt being a boy or a girl would have any bearing on their opportunities. Finally, I asked whether they saw any obstacles towards the goal of true gender equality.

Their answers were consistent – here are some extracts.

Thoughts from the Morrissey children

Fitz, 26

'As far as the role reversal is concerned, dad has always been a really stable presence, he's intellectually provocative, a good person to chat to and share things with. It was great for me that he was able to come to my matches, the other boys often had their mothers there, which was good but I really loved having my father there. It's given me a sense of what to aspire to as a man, dad's been a great role model for me in that sense and you have been a role model in other senses, you have shown me it's possible to achieve so much by sheer force of will power, by your desire to make a difference. I do think that seems more noticeable because you're a woman, perhaps we wouldn't have been so aware of it if you were a man.

'I think the experience of having lots of brothers and sisters has also influenced my perceptions of gender issues; everyone, girl or boy, has their own talents, but the girls and boys have different types of emotional needs. It's great to be part of a diverse group of people with our own talents – there's a certain creative synergy between us. For me as the eldest I've liked having a sense of responsibility and leadership and the awareness that I'm something of a role model for the younger ones. Inevitably, you and dad have had to adopt a slightly more laissez faire approach because there are so many of us. That has given us the space and freedom to create our own path, to follow our own things, to make our own choices.'

Clara, 17

'Having the traditional parent roles reversed means that we are encouraged to pursue our own interests and take risks regardless of gender norms or other people's perceptions. But it can also mean that sometimes I don't see you as much as I would like to.

'My impression is that being a girl might make it slightly harder to be taken seriously. There's a lot of emphasis on the issue in the media which perhaps makes it seem quite difficult for girls, but actually I am not so sure there is enough emphasis on preparing us well at school. I think the biggest obstacle to achieving gender equality is girls' lack of confidence, together with people in power not really seeing the need to change, or perhaps not wanting to change.'

Octavia, 14

'Having a mum and dad doing things differently shows that both men and women can do the same roles, have the same positions, it has influenced me, there are quite a lot of people in my year at school whose dads stay at home, you can do either or both. Having so many brothers and sisters has also shown me that people can do lots of different things and it's not about their gender but about what they can do, for example Flo is a singer and that is because she's good at that.

'Some people seem to think that girls might not be able to do certain things, that they're not capable of having a lot of power, or making good decisions. But I think that reflects a male view of what power is, and that view is changing. When people think of who's in charge, many people think of men, because that's the way they have known things to be. As more women become involved that will change.'

Tuppy, 19

'At school, particularly when I was very young, almost everyone else's dads were working rather than their mums, so I was always conscious that our family was different. I remember one of my teachers asking us all what our parents did and I was the only one whose mother was the breadwinner. As I went through school, my friends' families became more diverse, and that included more of the mothers working. It's just become more normal. I don't feel that this means there's less likelihood of me succeeding in my own career as a man, it's just going to be more equal than for previous generations. I expect my sisters and female friends will mostly have careers; actually, the girls I know at university often seem more driven than the boys – for example, they focus on securing internships.

'As far as obstacles to achieving equality are concerned, the workplace obviously still has its problems in terms of companies providing men and women with equal opportunities but I think those kinds of issues are being addressed more effectively than those relating to the perception of women – not just in terms of how men view women, but also how women view themselves. When I was talking to a few friends recently about the gender pay gap, one girl said that talkative boys are described as confident, whereas talkative girls are considered loud (i.e. annoying). Obviously there's more to confidence than how much noise you make, but societal views like this can make girls feel that it's not their place to be assertive and lead from the front. Whilst a girl can try to be more confident and strive for success, I can imagine that feels pretty daunting when many men and women of older generations have narrow-minded perceptions of how girls should behave and carry themselves.'

Cecily, 10

'The boys sometimes want to do different things than us, so it sometimes takes us longer to work out how to do something all together. Dad's really good at running the house but it's nice when you're at home. Dad's good at getting us to school and places on time.

'We don't talk about equality much at school but I would like us to. Lots of girls at school aren't very confident and we need to solve that.'

Millie, 18

'Having parents that challenge the stereotypes of male and female roles has shown me that "role reversal" is not only possible but it works. In our family we all depend on each other. And living side by side with so many people of the opposite sex has allowed me to appreciate our different qualities, but also made clear to me that we have a lot in common and we should be taking advantage of both our differences and the similarities. If I didn't have so many brothers – and sisters – I don't think I would be able to appreciate other people's ways of thinking as much. We have had to learn to get on well and interact with lots of people and to work in a team. We have to act selflessly and appreciate everyone's distinct skills and personalities.

'I think a lot of people talk about gender equality and its importance but few people put it into practice. People make subconscious assumptions and having brothers and sisters has made me realise that sometimes we act "like girls" or "like boys" but also we are all individuals and we can explore what actually interests us.'

Bea, 8

'I have seen you and dad do things differently from other parents but also there are other dads who collect people from school too and some of the other mothers work [her best friend's mother is a successful barrister]. We never really talk about girls and equality at school, but I hear about it at home. In the olden days boys got to do more things and girls didn't get to do so much and that needed to change and most of it has changed but not all of it, so things are not yet equal. People might think men are more powerful but sometimes women can be better.

'I think I will be good at running a business. I think I will be a good boss because I like to stand up for myself and to be in charge sometimes and to do what I want when I want to. I don't think it will make a big difference that I am a girl.'

Theo, 12

'I think having a mum who works and a dad at home has influenced me. I can clearly see that men and women can both achieve great things. If you didn't work, people might tell me that men and women cannot both achieve things. But I can see that many people in our family are achieving a lot, it doesn't matter what gender they are. Tuppy has written a book, you are helping women who want to work, and you have worked very hard and you are writing a book, Flo is an excellent singer, Fitzie is doing a PhD, dad has looked after us while you were at work and researched etc. There are many different interesting and wonderful people in our family and it seems odd that there aren't more families like us. I don't think our gender should make any difference to whether we succeed or not. The biggest obstruction to achieving equality between men and women is that not everyone agrees with everyone else. We live in a world where there are always some people with different opinions to others. We live in an argumentative world and that sometimes gets in the way of just making things better for everyone.'

As well as noting the complementary nature of their siblings' skills, the children have – through necessity – learned the value of teamwork. One evening when Richard and I were about to go out I heard the seven children who were at home arguing over which film to watch. They each wanted something different. I listened at the door, about to intervene, when I realised they were introducing a voting system. Each child had a first and second vote and after a number of voting rounds, they settled on *Ice Age*, all happy and seeming to have forgotten that only one of them had wanted that in the first place. It was lovely to realise that they had devised their own solution, working as a team. (And it made me think again about the benefits of proportional representation.) They also overcame any initial dominance by the eldest boy in the group – who had come up with the voting idea, but who in the end did not get his own choice (and accepted the outcome quite happily).

My eldest daughter Florence came home once from being interviewed about her music by a national newspaper. She casually mentioned over supper that they had asked her a lot about me. I gulped: this wasn't something we had ever discussed or 'rehearsed' and I wondered what she had said. When the article came out it was encouraging to read her comments. She said I had given her an appreciation for 'doing the thing and not holding back. It's sad when women feel they have to choose between being a housewife or succeeding in their career. When women give themselves over completely to their children it is amazing but it can also be inspiring for the children when mothers can juggle working and family. My mum would never say it but she is a great example of someone who can do both. She is special because she is my mum but it shows that anyone can do it.'

Florence is absolutely right that anyone can do it. Diversity and inclusion begin at home.

Chapter 9

Gender equality: good news for men and boys too

Oh, it's delightful to have ambitions. I'm so glad I have such a lot. And there never seems to be any end to them – that's the best of it. Just as soon as you attain to one ambition you see another one glittering higher up still. It does make life so interesting.

ANNE OF GREEN GABLES – L. M. MONTGOMERY

Quoting from *Anne of Green Gables* may seem an odd way to introduce a chapter on men and boys, but our ambition here is for two-way gender equality, a more 'glittering' and 'higher up' goal than a sole focus on women and girls. Richard has always maintained that the logical extension of the efforts to create greater opportunities for women is that men will have more choices, too. It's not a zero-sum game. But we still have narrow preconceptions about the role men should play: I was reminded of this when I asked our middle son Tuppy (then aged eight) what he wanted to do when he grew up and was momentarily taken aback by his answer, 'I think I'll stay at home like dad.'

The role of men in society has long been to focus on developing their careers, gain status and influence, provide financially for their families, and offer 'security' as the family leader, the patriarch. That sounds blatantly old-fashioned, but the reality is that while men are now expected to participate more in family and domestic life, those are more additional than replacement expectations. How many times have you spotted 'weekend dads' (just as I might be perceived as a weekend mum), clearly 'alpha men', pushing buggies, taking older children to the park, throwing themselves into their fatherhood responsibilities with great gusto at the end of a long working week, often alone, presumably to give their wives and partners a break.

It's difficult for men, too, to work out how to be modern, to be 'sensitive', yet also relevant and successful when that is defined quite narrowly in terms of status, earnings and power. I see many men genuinely desirous of change for women – often men with daughters are particularly committed – but it does leave a question mark hanging over their own place in the world that is not always easy to deal with.

My husband stopped working full time in 1999, long before the current wave of intense focus on gender equality. He is a private person and understandably reluctant to have his observations and experiences used for 'entertainment' purposes (there have been lots of opportunities to go on the radio or TV but to date he has turned them down because they seemed more for show than to help others). His perspective is an essential aspect of our family life and important to me and the children as individuals. His experiences have also foreshadowed the (incomplete as yet) evolution of thinking about how all our roles are in flux. We are now looking less at role reversal and more at sharing different aspects of what it takes to bring up a family, earn money and develop careers. The sharing arrangement is not static, either, but likely to vary from one stage of our lives to another.

Rather than making you hear my interpretation of Richard's views, he agreed to answer some questions directly. Before you read what he has to say I want to pay him a very big tribute. Richard volunteered to do what he does, but he needn't have made that move. He has a First Class Philosophy degree (something that eluded me) from Trinity College Dublin and is incredibly well read. He would say, modestly, that's because he has more time than most people, which is an interesting thought in itself – why are people too busy to read? He has a powerful set of messages and ideas about his experiences to convey, and I am grateful to him for sharing them.

H: It was an unusual step to offer to go freelance and play a bigger role in the upbringing of our children – what were your reasons for doing that?

R: At the time I felt as if I had completed my current career path, which is unusual as I was only 35. But I experienced a strong pull to start afresh and live a different kind of life – one where I could contribute to our family in a more meaningful way and be more true to myself. In itself, freelancing was not then and is not now unusual for a man, but I did think at the time it might be a means of transitioning to a different path. It was obvious to me that I had reached a ceiling in terms of what I could achieve in journalism, intellectually and financially, whereas your path was much more open-ended, with fewer limits and greater potential earning power.

H: Are you happy with the way it worked out, for you (rather than the impact on me or the family)?

R: Yes, I am happy with how it has worked out for me, but I can't really separate 'me' from how it has worked out for you and the family. Judging success or happiness involves many factors, and the happiness of others is very important to me, so I am happy when I feel I have been a positive and supportive influence for our family together. However, with the children now growing up and starting to move on I feel I must consider how I might do things differently over the next few years. There is a time for everything and it's important to know when to make changes. It will be twenty years of this life soon, so I feel I need to explore what's next. It feels poignant seeing the children moving on so I need to ensure there is not a vacuum in my life. You and the children are my life, so that is a big thing and I need to work with it.

H: What are the aspects you haven't enjoyed?

R: It has felt lonely at times – it's as if I'm living between two worlds. I'm neither a housewife with friends and a yoga practice nor a man in the public domain working and earning a living and playing golf with colleagues. And yes, it has sometimes been aggravating and frustrating for me. I have felt a mismatch between my insights and my capacity to use that in the world outside our family. I have been helped by being able to help you (and some others) feel the power within and be in turn a happier person. So it's not that I don't enjoy what I do, it is more that it feels like I am less defined and conventional so I have to explain or account for myself to people who don't know me. That can be tedious. But it's not a big deal in the scheme of things.

H: Do you think our arrangements have been beneficial for the children? For the family as a whole? What have been the challenges?

R: Yes, I do think our arrangements have been beneficial – very beneficial. I think the children are good-hearted people and well balanced (mostly!) and they are happy. I feel we both have provided them with great stability and a feeling they have our support to find their own way in life without being too controlled or driven by us. They have the space to make mistakes without the world falling in on them. I think it has been valuable for them to know that with you at work I am always around and keep a relatively stable and balanced environment for all of us. I have initiated various routines over the years – 'cocktail time' (before you call social services, this is actually crisps and raw vegetables at 5 p.m. served in a special segmented bowl), 'sitting down time' (our shorthand for saying enough jumping around, time to gather quietly on the sofa), the repetitive airing of favourite TV shows – *Dad's Army*, *Jeeves and Wooster*, *Modern Family*, rituals like joining in 'the clap' in the *Friends* introductory theme tune, and so on. That's provided some certainty for the children over many years, and a sense of belonging, in a world that can be very unsettling and confusing.

H: Are you surprised that nearly two decades later you are still one of the very few men we know who has a 'non-traditional' role? Why do you think it's proving so hard to shift expectations about how men and women should spend their lives?

R: I'm not surprised but it is more nuanced than it was twenty years ago. There are more men working in flexible jobs and who are self-employed so that allows them to be more involved with their family, which is a positive. But there are not many men who 'just' look after the family. Even I tell people 'I'm also a meditation teacher'. I think being a parent in our society is not seen as a meaningful full-time role, especially for a man, given the lack of income. Our society is driven by 'wins', striving, pushing forward, public success, and this success is often measured by financial power. Our world has to date been very vertical, not horizontal – I'm horizontal. That may be changing with the next generation of both boys and girls expecting something different, with technology broadening power across networks rather than it being from top to bottom. I think people are happier and more productive when there is less hierarchy – and I'm sure our children will be able to work like that. Companies are seeing that flatter structures make more sense today.

We live in a very public world and being at home is more a private, secluded place now, especially as many women also work. So the people who are at home are a smaller group than in the past. In other words, the role, already rather subordinate in the eyes of many, is diminishing in importance. It's certainly not seen as being in any way powerful (even though we play a big role in bringing up the next generation, which is in its way quite a responsibility) and that's harder for men when we are conditioned to 'make our way in the world'. And of course, in the recent past, and in traditional societies today, being at home is still associated with women and mothers. There is change here in the UK but in many parts of the world things remain as they were.

H: Only a tiny proportion (1 in 100) of men took up shared parental leave in the first year it was available. Of those who did, 51% said they risked being viewed as 'less of a man'. How can we encourage broader definitions of masculine identity and success?

R: Whether we like it or not, men automatically associate themselves with the traditional role of 'going out to work'. That is the base case scenario for most men. More women now have careers too, but there is I suspect a sense of optionality for middle-class, more affluent women, that they can always decide to put family first. Other women need to work, it's a financial necessity, but for different reasons they may feel it's less about having a career for themselves than providing for their family. They are a mother or a woman first. Men of my generation haven't really felt they have a choice other than working for their entire adult life until retirement, and we've also been brought up to believe our success is inextricably linked to our careers. That is difficult to change. I think if male leaders took parental leave that would encourage others but again this is difficult for many men, as they will be concerned they will lose out to the competition. Think of many of the senior men you know and you will see how strange it would be for them to opt for the leave as a woman would. Staying at home with a baby and 'missing in action'? I think part of the issue is that many 'successful' businessmen actually feel quite insecure, as well as competitive. They are simply not willing to risk losing out in a world they feel committed to, and many of them were not brought up to develop their nurturing side. They may be happy to support these initiatives once they've 'made it' but on the way up it is harder to step back and stay at home.

These rather fixed attitudes are not just affecting the workplace and families but our approach to solving societal problems. Success has so often been perceived to be about taking a very 'strong' stance, an aggressive, uncompromising position. That is a masculine version of events. I heard a great speech at our daughter Millie's school speech day, by Dr Eve Poole who teaches 'leadership and character' at Ashridge Executive Education, formerly Ashridge Business School. Dr Poole reminded us – though surely we shouldn't need reminding – that we don't exactly live in caves any more, that the fighting mentality is yesteryear, or at least only useful occasionally. We don't need to be in a constant state of alert, ready to attack. You have been successful through being more 'tend and befriend', nurturing rather than railing against, and there are many more situations now, not just in business, obviously, where we need more of that approach. We need to be less aggressive. We need more women to be comfortable bringing their femininity to the fore, to shift our overall approach to something gentler, more nuanced, more sensitive.

H: What do you think needs to happen or what would you like to see to create a more balanced and more open society?

R: My hope is that the changing nature of the workplace and the speedy advance of robotics and artificial intelligence will make rethinking how we live a necessity. There just won't be a choice but to change. There is likely to be huge disruption ahead so we need to work out now how we can guide the future or at least plan for various outcomes. When men can feel that their work and their life are not separate and that we can look first at how we live and then work out how and when we need to work – then we will be making real progress.

Perhaps we may find different kinds of approach unfolding – maybe a group of men and women who are very creative, and develop a new social contract, along the lines suggested by R. Buckminster Fuller that 'One in ten thousand of us can make a technological breakthrough capable of supporting all the rest.' That may sound radical, but we have internet billionaires who are highly philanthropic today; it's far from inconceivable that we can come up with a societal model that reflects how much progress we have made rather than simply builds on the structure that – sometimes – worked in the past.

H: Do you think the different ways we educate boys and girls perpetuates the imbalance?

R: The education system is where we can start showing all young people how their future life/work can be more nuanced than just getting a job and working your way up. As things stand, the work model is primarily a masculine large public/private global firm with a fixed, vertical hierarchy. Although there are thousands of companies not like that, this is seen as the norm. It is the working template. People can be educated together (important this is both male and female) to show we can have different paths, all valid, but each having their own consequences, and of course they will have different outcomes for the employees and perhaps financially.

From experiences with our own children, we've seen that girls' schooling can sometimes – unintentionally – reinforce the girls' insecurities, while boys' schooling needs to evolve to equip men for more possibilities than a linear career. Perhaps surprisingly, that's particularly true of single-sex education. The best schools are aware of this of course, but still there's a tendency to fall back on previously tried-and-tested approaches that may not work so well in future. Schools, parents, the media, governments, have a tendency to compare girls with boys, women with men, trying to fit the women into the men's template, which will never lead to equality and happiness. Women shouldn't feel under any pressure to copy men and men shouldn't feel pressured to live like their fathers. The change will come when it happens for both men and women and when we all start to learn that we have options to live differently.

H: Do you worry about positive discrimination affecting our sons? I see growing prejudice towards privately (and highly) educated white, middle-class men, a really unfortunate and contradictory consequence of efforts to create equality. The point, surely, is not to replace one form of injustice with another.

R: I don't worry about positive discrimination on a personal level. I think the boys are able to demonstrate what they have to offer and if they are discriminated against, I'd suggest that company or institution isn't necessarily one that they should get involved with anyway. I do think positive discrimination occurs at present, however. It is, I hope, a temporary issue and occurs where people are getting the means of change wrong by remaining biased and focusing on duality (men/women, black/white, gay/straight) rather than looking at the issue from the perspective of the whole. The current rather adolescent 'identity politics' approach will fail but, again, the education system is currently driving this identity mentality, along with much of the media, and we need to evolve, to move on from this simplistic and divisive way of looking at things.

H: Is the present approach taken by many women to achieve gender equality a good one? What would you recommend we do differently?

R: As I've said, the current approach won't work out, as it is primarily focusing on the other side (women, LGBT, ethnic minorities, etc.) instead of looking at it from a unified point of view. Women do this too, and definitely shouldn't protest or complain or blame men when so many of us want to see progress, for our daughters but also our wives, our sisters, our friends. We're only going to make that progress if we work together. You did that with the 30% Club but that just gives us a clue as to how much more can be achieved. The aim behind our efforts has to be to try to create better outcomes for *all* humans, not separate groups. We have to move on from our tendency to try to help the discriminated-against group while leaving the old work model and indeed old life model untouched. We have been doing things in the name of diversity – necessary to get the focus at first – that now should be done in the name of creating better ways of working and living.

We have been trying to get others a seat at the men's table when we should be questioning whether this is the right table and if it's worth sitting at.

So we need to be more ambitious; I know we both believe that now is the moment when people are seeing what's wrong with what we have at present. We need balance and harmony and that isn't what we have today. I think that's a goal that can unify us.

*

In 2018, Business in the Community embarked on a study aptly titled 'Equal Lives', specifically to explore the experiences of fathers and male carers in the workplace. After all the research into women's perspectives, we felt that the experience of men needed further investigation – and greater exposure. The research comprised two elements: over 10,000 survey responses, and a series of interviews and focus groups. There were many interesting findings; the standout being the confirmation that men want to play a bigger role in caring while often struggling to do so. The reasons cited vary: work expectations (even when organisations offer family-friendly policies, there is a reluctance to take them up for fear of damaging career prospects or job security), societal pressures (what does it mean to 'be a man' today?) or couples' own behaviours (there's still a tendency to fall into traditional roles once they have caring responsibilities). Fathers in same sex-relationships offered valuable insights and a possible solution to that last problem: these men felt they had naturally settled into a shared set of responsibilities when it came to caring for their children alongside their careers. One partner tended to take the 'lead' role as carer, the other was more focused on his career, but they each felt they could realise their personal preference. Compared with heterosexual couples, the decision process was less influenced by external factors, including societal pressures and norms and the expectations of their employers or managers, and more by what each partner actually wanted to do. It seems so obvious, really – and there's nothing actually stopping the rest of us from doing the same; we just need to focus more on what works for us and our families rather than what others might think.

My elder two sons are at Oxford University, both linguists, one a Prize Fellow of All Souls specialising in

Arabic and Islamic Studies and the other a modern languages undergraduate (French and German). I gave a lecture on gender equality at the Oxford Union a few years ago and was surprised that there were as many young men in the audience as young women. I was a bit worried they thought I was there to talk about something else, so I checked quietly with one student, who assured me that he knew what I was there to discuss and actually he had brought along his girlfriend, since he thought they could both benefit from the talk.

Unsurprisingly, my sons were the only two men who came along to hear me present to the Oxford Women in Business Society more recently (I also speak at other universities). As usual, I gave a short account of my own career, including the highlights and low points, the experience of the 30% Club and my tips for success, including a number of family anecdotes that I'm sure were slightly embarrassing for Fitz and Tuppy (they handled it well). Like me, my sons were intrigued by the questions that arose, many of which overlapped with the 'top ten' in Chapter 7. Away from the lecture room and the college bar, these young women seemed to feel surprisingly insecure about their futures.

Fitz offered his thoughts:

'I feel girls of my generation tend to have one of two quite differing positions about their futures. Most of the girls I know are assertive and behave as if they don't see any barriers to what they hope to achieve in life, they have intellectually and academically done as well as if not better than their male peers. I also hope and think that men of my generation have more enlightened views towards women than previous generations and that's recognised by these women. I do think that most girls don't in any way feel that men are preventing them from getting where they want to, but there is another smaller group who push a victimhood narrative. These are women on the lookout for offence and they wouldn't want to recognise the positive progress. They are a small but vocal minority, and not like the women who came to your talk who are focused on their future, who are hard-working and also often involved in sports – they enjoy university life and see the opportunities, and one thing we should be aware of is that this quieter majority may get drowned out by the vocal minority that I think is growing.

'While you were speaking at the Women in Business event, it struck me that there would never be the male equivalent, and those questions would also never arise if it was a generic business event either – people, men or women, wouldn't ask about, say, the impact of children on their careers. I think the forum gave women the chance to ask those questions that they might not usually feel comfortable asking: you were speaking as someone who's been where they want to go to and you show your vulnerability, what can go wrong as well as the successes. I think that draws out these real questions that girls have, which is interesting.'

Fitz's younger sister Florence was not at that talk but I was intrigued that she offered similar observations about how the approach being taken by some young women may actually impede their progress:

'I think the biggest impediments to achieving full gender equality are the media and tradition. With the mass of technology at our fingertips – Instagram, Facebook, Twitter, the news, magazines and brands – it is hard to have one clear-cut message out there and the lines around what is "correct" and "inclusive" are blurred. I see many women my age [22] posting about feminism on their Instagrams in an aggressive and counterproductive way – not on purpose but because we haven't been told any other way to get the message across than the way the men have … through force or revolt, rather than by taking action as women. We need to speak out, but not in the current way. I hope that we can focus on using platforms like Rookie magazine (a teenage girl zine created by blogger Tavi Gevinson) and other collectives that allow men to be part of them too. We need to see that we need each other – now more than ever. Otherwise the gap and the alienation will continue on both sides. We need more of the understanding of togetherness, rather than women alone fighting for themselves.'

I love Florence's reference to *acting as women*. After that Oxford Women in Business talk, one young woman shared her experience of being a summer intern at a bank. At the end of the programme, she was asked to assess her performance and in particular to explain what skills she thought she had brought to the team. She felt the need to comply with convention, to emphasise how she had been applying her mathematical skills, the hours she had been working, how she had taken instruction well and completed her tasks. In reality, she thought her emotional intelligence, ability to collaborate and to listen, those feminine qualities we have talked so much about, had really helped the team to work well together. Her dilemma was that it felt risky to emphasise this, that the company wasn't yet ready to value those differences, that they seemed 'soft', and she would be undermining her chances of securing a permanent position. My challenge back was: would she want actually to join the company if that was true?

We can all see that this is unfinished business.

Chapter 10

Women, money and power

'I truly believe that women should be financially independent from their men. Let's face it, money gives men the power to run the show. It gives men the power to define value ... it's ridiculous.'

BEYONCÉ

Women have an ambivalent relationship with money. Culturally it's an awkward, even embarrassing, subject. Of course, we like the freedom and choice that money gives us, but while we might happily discuss topics as wide-ranging as politics, relationships, work, health and fashion with our friends, financial issues are something of a taboo. While women often control a large proportion of regular household spending, many delegate longer-term financial planning to 'their men', as Beyoncé puts it. When was the last time *you* discussed your general financial well-being, how to make your money grow or how to save for a pension?

The problem is, *not* talking about something often means not dealing with it – and not properly dealing with money undermines women in a very basic way. If we want true equality, we should be looking after our financial well-being in the same way that we look after our physical and mental health, our careers, homes and relationships. It's not about being materialistic; it's about being empowered, having options, being able to use our time the way we want to and – critically – avoiding vulnerability or hardship. Financial capability is an important aspect of women's ability to control our destiny, to *own the process* as we discussed in Chapter 7, and to become partners with men rather than supplicants.

At present, our lack of engagement with the topic puts us at a significant disadvantage, and one that tends to increase with age. 'Insuring Women's Futures' is a programme established by the UK insurance industry aimed at helping women become more financially resilient. Its 2017 publication, 'Securing the Financial Future of the Next Generation', makes for sobering reading. The report highlights six 'moments that matter' – life stages such as entering the workplace or becoming a mother – where women are particularly exposed to financial risks. Poor outcomes at these 'moments' all too frequently accumulate over a woman's lifetime, to devastating effect. The most shocking statistic in the report relates to pensions: by the time the average British woman reaches the age of 65, her pension pot is only one fifth of the value of the average man's. Not 20% *less than* but 20% *of* men's retirement provision. Coupled with higher life expectancy (in the UK, a 65-year-old man can expect to live for another eighteen and a half years compared with twenty-one years for women), this leaves many women financially fragile and especially vulnerable to hardship in their old age. We can't do anything about getting older, but we can do something about getting poorer.

Closing the gender pay gap by equalising women's career opportunities is an important part of equalising wealth and the power that comes with it, but we need to take other steps as well. Wealth is a product of what we earn, spend and how we invest, so we also need to learn how to spend wisely and close the *gender investment gap*.

But before we have any real hope of doing that, money has to feel relevant and interesting, something that we *do* talk about and are confident we can master. Finance needs to be integral to our lives, so we can lead better lives. Taking an active, prevention-is-better-than-cure approach is key. Speaking to her granddaughter, one of Legal and General's pensioner customers captured it beautifully and spontaneously: 'If you get it right, dear, retirement is a future full of Saturdays.' (When we played a video of their chat at a client conference, the immediate reaction around the room was: 'I spend a lot of money on Saturdays!')

So, what's stopping women taking control of their finances? Many studies identify similar reasons for women's disengagement with money. A 2018 report, 'The Financial Power of Women' published by Fidelity International, cites a familiar list: female respondents describe the topic as complicated, intimidating and incomprehensible and the sales process as aggressive, patronising and exclusive; we don't feel we have the right information or knowledge to make a good decision – and we don't trust financial services companies. When we save, we end up being 'recklessly cautious', keeping our money in cash rather than aiming for higher long-term growth through investments. According to government figures, 5.2 million women subscribed to cash ISAs (tax-exempt Individual Savings Accounts) in 2015–16 compared with 4.4 million men, but over 1.1 million men bought stocks and shares ISAs compared with less than 900,000 women.

Many companies have been trying to attract female investors but a quick look at their marketing literature reveals a problem that will by now sound familiar: the language and approach are usually standardised around what works for men. It's ironic, since many marketing professionals are women, but as we've seen in gender equality efforts more broadly, the (flawed) tendency is to make incremental adjustments to techniques that have worked for men, rather than radically rethink how to reach a new audience. The marketing world has developed its own vocabulary, measuring success according to 'KPIs' (Key Performance Indicators) and clinical measures around the 'cost of acquisition' of customers. It's a framework that might provide reference points and a means of assessing results, but it won't help us capture those moments when we need to *think differently*. If we're trying to reach those that haven't been motivated to invest before, it seems obvious that we need to start over. In what I hope will now be a familiar refrain, if we really want to see more women investing, we need to feel confident enough to ditch the spreadsheet and develop a new vision – and to experiment more. To test and learn so we can find out what actually works.

Former investment banker Andrea Turner Moffitt was struggling with her own relationship with investing, and through comparing notes with friends – similarly well-educated, professional women – discovered she was far from alone. She turned her discussions into a comprehensive, global study of the investment habits of (relatively high-earning) women from New York to London to Hong Kong – I took part in a London focus group. The results are documented in *Harness the Power of the Purse: Winning Women Investors* and the messages are clear. Talking amongst ourselves, women stress that we want to be understood first, to have someone listen to our financial hopes and fears, before anyone tries to sell us anything. The sales pitch itself can be a complete turn-off. We tend to be less interested than men in making money for its own sake; specific goals motivate us more, such as paying for our children's education, paying off our mortgage or feeling financially secure. Women and millennials (of both sexes) are also anxious to ensure our money has a positive impact – we don't want to line the pockets of those who are out for themselves, harm the environment, treat their employees badly or don't support the women who work for them. We feel sceptical that our money will be put to good use.

This all adds up to what might seem like a big set of challenges. But perhaps it's really quite simple. To put it bluntly, many women find money 'boring'. They need to feel a desire to get involved, and won't be persuaded if they are simply told it will be 'good for them'. Zoe Lyons is a talented comedian who performed at the inaugural 2018 Women in Pensions Awards: during her act, she confessed that at the age of forty-six she still hadn't done anything about a pension. 'Is it too late?' she asked, feigning worry, before quickly acknowledging that though she knew she should, she couldn't be bothered. The subject just wasn't exciting enough.

I took part in *The Lens*, a Business in the Community podcast that brings together different generational perspectives around key topics. Presenter and self-proclaimed 'connector' Oli Barrett interviewed me alongside a much younger woman, Kristy McKenzie, engagement manager at The Bakery, which partners big brands and corporations with tech start-ups. I asked Kristy, who is articulate, intelligent and has carefully managed her early career, about her attitudes to money. She explained that she had started saving for a deposit on a flat, realising it would be liberating to own her own home. She had reached the conclusion that the only way to make her savings grow was to invest, so she'd taken out a stocks and shares ISA. All great to hear. But at the same time, Kristy said she didn't 'feel educated or confident enough to make investment decisions' and had ended up delegating to an adviser, still feeling unsure if she'd done the right thing. When I asked if she had discussed any of this with her friends she said no, that the subject of money only came up if one of her friends was to say something like, 'I can't go to the pub tonight because I don't have any money'. Yet she could see they could *all* benefit from comparing notes, encouraging each other and sharing what financial knowledge they possessed. So why not? Kristy's straightforward explanation corroborated the 'boring' theory: 'Money is not as entertaining a topic as, say, travel or music. People don't want to talk about things that are "sensible".'

How can we make the subject less tedious, more scintillating? There are precedents. During our podcast, Oli mentioned that in the 1960s, police would stop joggers in the street, questioning their 'suspicious' activity. Health 'fanatics' were viewed as eccentric. Drinking what would now be considered copious quantities of alcohol – even during the working day – was the norm, along with a smoking habit. Since then, it's not just jogging that's taken off; very many of us do fitness classes, go to the gym or simply count our daily steps and monitor our sleep using an activity tracker. We are *aware* of the importance of exercise, good diet and sleep habits, and even if we're not always virtuous, we try to indulge only in moderation. Fitness has become a subject we *do* talk about; I have just passed two male colleagues on their way to the gym comparing notes about what muscles they are going to work on today, having previously overheard two female colleagues talking about the nutritional value of their respective lunches. Personally, although I am (too) busy *and* it's something of a cliché for women my age, I make time to do Pilates classes for both physical stamina and mental alertness – the complicated exercises help me to focus only on that moment. After many failed attempts, mostly involving more competitive fitness classes, I finally found what works for me and try to go to the sessions even when I'm feeling lazy or particularly time-pressured – because I know I'll feel better afterwards. In the long term, we know our bodies and minds will benefit, so we're willing to make short-term sacrifices.

The lens through which we look at physical (and now mental) fitness has shifted: what once seemed boring, irrelevant or odd has simply become *what we do*.

I believe we can – and must – do the same when it comes to finance. To safeguard our financial health and security, we must create an *investment generation*, and specifically a generation of female investors, entrepreneurs and business owners. Arguably the closest we've come to creating excitement about investing is the Bitcoin craze – where WhatsApp groups have shared 'tips', and it's been seen to be cool (though risky) to get involved. I'm advocating something less speculative, but potentially just as exciting. What I love about investing is that you can put your money where your mouth is. Investing in companies means that you own a (small) part of them. Collectively, investors can therefore influence what the company does when it comes to the environment, its workforce, the community and, of course, its customers. We could speed up action on climate change, for example, if we all decided *not* to invest in the worst-polluting companies and instead invested in businesses working to create sources of clean energy. Worried about plastic in the ocean? We know we can stop using plastic bags and straws – but we can also invest in companies that are doing the most to reduce the use of plastic. Want to drive gender equality? We can invest more in those companies that are doing the right things for the women in their workforce. Investing can be about more than 'just' financial returns – even small amounts of money can be pooled together to create a positive impact on the world. (And don't imagine you have to choose between profit and purpose – would you want to invest in an auto manufacturer that isn't researching electric or hybrid cars today? Sustainably managed companies are also well positioned to deliver sustainable returns.)

Still, even when their interest is ignited, women often ask me, 'How do I get started?' Like many things we're curious about today, the internet is a good place to begin. It's important to find a neutral, impartial 'tutor', such as (in the UK) the Money Advice Service which gives free guidance on the basics. The text is straightforward – but it's not, to use our word, scintillating. I am excited by a new campaign, 'Financially Fabulous', launched in June 2018 by Hearst magazines, publishers of a wide range of women's titles, including *Red*, *Good Housekeeping* and

Cosmopolitan. If you haven't come across it, look it up – the initiative includes a fortnightly email, pages in the monthly magazines devoted to real-life money issues and events like 'Speed Date a Money Expert'.

'Boring Money' is the actual name of a business that specialises in 'helping normal people' cut through the jargon around investing and gives them the tools and the confidence to get started. Legal and General partnered with founder Holly Mackay and her team to try to solve the breakdown in communications between the financial industry and 'normal people'. Seven (female) communications experts, including a columnist for a Sunday magazine and a TV presenter, reviewed existing 'unfathomable' material from financial companies and 'translated' them into concepts that became an art exhibition. For example, a portfolio statement, originally a dull-looking series of lines of text, with weightings of each company in percentages, was transformed into this very simple, clear summary of familiar company logos, with the size of each position reflected in the size of the rectangle on the grid.

It was fascinating seeing people's reactions to the exhibits. The opening piece was deliberately interactive – asking, 'What are you investing for?' and inviting attendees to jot down their financial goals, write or draw their hopes and dreams. And the visual portfolio statement got people talking about what companies they *wouldn't* personally want to invest in – oil, tobacco and drinks companies were often cited – along with some surprise that this portfolio, where allocations were simply made on the basis of company size, was so heavily skewed towards these areas. These 'index' funds are the cheapest to invest in – but it soon became clear that once people became aware of what their money would be used for, they wanted to explore alternatives. The simple graphic brought the subject alive; the attendees had a view and were keen to get involved.

The medium-term solution is to educate our children (both boys and girls) better and earlier about money. Financial education became part of the secondary school

curriculum in England in September 2014, mandatory for pupils between the ages of eleven and sixteen. The syllabus is designed to cover both day-to-day money management and financial planning, so it includes budgeting, managing risk, insurance, savings and pensions, credit and debt, and financial products. Implementation has been tricky, however, with teachers reporting a lack of confidence in their expertise and the quality of the teaching materials, and feeling limited by time, resources and competing priorities.

As in other areas of change, we need multiple efforts by many people to create real impact, and to share responsibility as parents, as pupils, across government and as employers. In the UK, a number of organisations – including The Money Charity, Young Money (a cross-party parliamentary initiative), KickStart Money (a collaboration between twenty leading savings and investment firms and MyBnk, a financial education charity) – are working hard to improve young people's financial literacy. There's a lot to do, but the programmes are leveraging what's been found to work in other areas. Mathletics, for example, is a wonderful tool used by many schools to make maths more 'real' and fun, using games and puzzles that are familiar to everyday life, rather than abstract concepts. The website describes the programme as a 'captivating' online learning space and I can confirm that even those of my children who struggle with maths enjoy the experience and the rewards they can achieve as they accomplish the tasks. Money can be brought to life in the same way – in fact, I'd say it's easier. My youngest daughter's obsession with making slime (in common with many girls her age) has catalysed a whole new level of interest in how to make her pocket money go further as she shops for 'ingredients', including glue, contact lens fluid, glitter and colouring.

Through her attempts to make the best (and most) slime for the keenest price, Bea has learned the importance of comparison shopping (and, when it comes to buying on the internet, checking postage costs and delivery times before proceeding) and she knows she gets a better deal when buying in bulk. We've entered into negotiations about advancing her pocket money (or she's done extra chores around the house to earn more) so that she can take advantage of temporary special deals, and I encourage her to save for bulk discounts. I've made a point of regularly asking her about the financial aspects of her hobby, and she seems to enjoy sharing all the savings she's made, or (less happily) complaining when she realises she's overpaid.

And I've started to extend the topic to other important issues. Bea is good about recycling packaging, and gets cross if a small bottle of glue arrives encased in a giant cardboard box. But she does also love glitter, so we've discussed how this is harmful to the environment and she's been experimenting with other ways to make her slime beautiful, with different colours and textures. We've discussed why she needs to wear thin rubber gloves when she's handling all the chemicals, and whether those gloves are environmentally friendly. In other words, I'm trying to channel her excitement about slime into areas where she might not be quite so focused.

It's a pretty simple – and frankly quite obvious – approach, but we need to work out how to scale it up. The UK Girlguiding organisation has nearly half a million current members and a staggering one in four British adult women is a former Brownie, Girl Guide or Ranger. (Whenever I ask any group of friends or colleagues, I've found we 'over-index' – it's more like one in three.) Recently, the organisation has overhauled its revered badges programme, modernising the topics to help equip girls for adult life today. Legal and General is sponsoring a new 'Saver' badge, where girls undertake fun activities designed to help them become financially savvy. Alongside this, we're launching a new competition, 'My Future Business', aimed at encouraging entrepreneurship amongst 10- to 14-year-old girls. As our collaboration develops, we're likely to launch other schemes such as investment clubs, mimicking the successful models in a number of private schools (in my experience, mostly boys' schools – my younger son in particular has developed a keen interest in investing through a club, where the art of picking strong companies is approached along the lines of the wildly successful fantasy football competition). All of these efforts – and more – are aimed at creating a level playing field between boys and girls and more awareness of money matters generally.

We need to address the gender wealth gap from every angle *and* at every age. Millennials (both male and female) are storing up financial problems earlier than previous generations. Someone born in the early 1980s in the UK is likely to be struggling to get on the property ladder and earning less at the same stage in life than someone born ten years before them. Those born a decade later have the added burden of high student debt. At the same time, surveys suggest that 'FOMO' (Fear of Missing Out) is leading to young people overspending to keep up with their friends.

But these are just the basics: we also want women to be great financial successes, to create their own wealth and really own their destiny, and be able to influence others positively, too, through philanthropy and other ways of giving back. Here we face further societal hurdles, as Candace Bushnell, author of *Sex and the City*, has suggested: 'Women with money and women in power are two uncomfortable ideas in our society.'

Jessica Knoll is the author of a bestselling novel, *Luckiest Girl Alive*, a work she originally insisted was fiction but later 'confessed' was based on her horrific experience of gang rape aged fifteen. In a *New York Times* op-ed, she wrote that the experience 'annotated my definition of success. I decided I could not consider myself successful unless I was somebody powerful, somebody nobody could hurt. Success became a means to wrest back control, literally to increase my value. There is a metonym for that: money.' The title of Jessica's article? 'I Want to Be Rich and I'm Not Sorry.'

In that piece – which went viral – Jessica spoke of her

ambition to be rich, along with a willingness to promote herself, and observed that these desires might be considered obnoxious, because she is a woman. She's right – but at the same time, her observation reveals a female habit that holds us back: we spend far too much time and energy *thinking about how we'll be perceived*. It is suggested, harshly, that 'we (women) are our own worst enemy' – I don't agree, but we do need to focus more on achieving our aims than on second-guessing what others will think – including when it comes to making money.

To achieve anything like richness, we need to encourage more female entrepreneurship. On the face of it, things look like they are improving if you are a woman starting or scaling up a business. In the US, women own more than 11.6 million firms – a jump of 114% over the past two decades. These businesses collectively employ more than 9 million workers and contribute US$1.7 trillion in revenues to the US economy. In the UK, record numbers of women are identifying as business owners, patent applications from female investors have increased, and revenues from women-owned enterprises are on the rise. But these relative gains are still not closing the *gender funding gap*.

In 2017, there was actually a small drop in the amount of funding granted to UK companies with at least one female founder compared with 2016, despite overall funding for entrepreneurs almost doubling over the same year. The statistics are stark: funding increased by 55% for male founders, while falling 0.1% for female founders. As a result, the proportion of all funding invested in British businesses with a female founder fell from 14.9% to 8.5% in 2017 from the previous year.

'The evidence is unequivocal: there is a growing disparity in funding between male and female entrepreneurs,' warns Sophie Jarvis, head of the Female Founders Forum. 'There is significant evidence to support the fact that the funding gap is influenced to a large extent by unconscious biases from investors to the detriment of women.'

A poll conducted for the *Telegraph*'s excellent Women Mean Business campaign revealed that 65% of women said they had been 'unfairly treated by financial services when trying to raise funding' and 72% had 'used their own credit cards, cash and savings to fund their businesses'. 41% of women said they 'didn't feel they were on an equal footing with men'.

In short, women are either set a higher bar or have to 'lean in' to raise funding. And yet our business ideas work out just as well as men's. The Boston Consulting Group studied the track record of US-based business start-ups and found that women 'ultimately deliver higher revenue – more than twice as much per dollar invested – than those founded by men', despite not receiving the same level of financial backing. It makes economic and investment sense to support female-founded firms.

The feedback suggests that – as usual – women looking for business funding are being evaluated *as if they were men*. As we've explored throughout this book, we have our own ways of doing things, our own ways of presenting ideas and behaving. These ways are neither inferior nor superior to men's – they are simply different. Just as we saw when it came to accelerating boardroom diversity, the definition of what 'good' looks like needs broadening so that different people can have their business ideas heard. There's a wearisome, déjà vu, chicken-and-egg problem: there are very few women in private equity and venture capitalism participating in the funding decisions. The British Venture Capital Association's 2018 Women in Private Equity study found that women make up just 14% of investment teams at private equity firms, and a mere 6% of senior investment professionals. The industry has been trying to recruit more women but progress is glacial. For now, these firms should consider adding more women to their investor panels from outside, such as those who have already succeeded as entrepreneurs.

In the meantime, this is one area where we can help ourselves through networks. Communities of female investors supporting smart businesses run by women is a great 'beat-them-in-the-market', win-win strategy. Groups – both large and small – have already been established on both sides of the Atlantic to encourage women to invest in each other's business ideas; examples include Female Funders, the AllBright Fund and the Female Founders Fund. Money talks, so their success – our success – will challenge and drive change in those 'biased' investors. Yet another example of how we can create a new system to help ourselves, rather than hit our heads upon the brick wall of the old. As we reach for gender equality, let's help each other become more financially empowered.

Chapter 11

We can write the future together

I am only one, but I am one. I cannot do everything, but I can do something. And I will not let what I cannot do interfere with what I can do.

EDWARD EVERETT HALE, AMERICAN AUTHOR,
HISTORIAN AND UNITARIAN MINISTER

This book is mostly about our great opportunity to achieve gender equality – but of course that is not a foregone conclusion. There are several risks to guard against. In my opinion, none of these specifically falls under the heading 'Donald Trump', whose election and subsequent actions and remarks have angered so many women. Anger is a natural reaction to offence – but being angry won't necessarily help us make further progress. That anger needs to be channelled into actions of our own that can move us forward. Today's gender equality movement has momentum because it chimes with the way our world is evolving – and one man, however big his job title, might slow us down but cannot turn back time.

I'm not complacent. There are a number of reasons why we might fall short of our goal of creating a new balanced society. Four of the key risks lie largely within women's own control:

1. We could lapse back into a 'gender war' mentality, provoked by #MeToo and #TimesUp;
2. We could focus on just one side of the gender equality equation – progress for women – and fail to address what it means for men;
3. We could miss the point by emulating men and boys rather than bringing our differences to the fore, and
4. We could fret that our efforts to 'complete the task' are self-indulgent, when there is so much still to do to secure basic protections for many women and girls.

There's a fifth, big threat, too. That the deep divisions in our society today, including the complex issues related to immigration, are seen as linked to our new appetite for tolerance and diversity – prompting a backlash.

Let's look at the first four risks before even trying to address the fifth.

Feminism has been a battle of the sexes for so long that it is sometimes hard to see that many men are now very much on our side – and to acknowledge and enjoy the progress we've been making. It has, for many, never been a better time to be a girl, yet highly educated, affluent women often dwell on the unresolved issues. It's important to keep working on those, but counterproductive if we complain more than we celebrate. There will always be 'retro' men, but there are many more who are concerned about backward steps too, and we need to continue to work together with our male allies. The reality is that the pivot point on the line of what is acceptable, what is the 'norm', has already shifted a long way – which is why rogue behaviours and misguided comments get so much criticism. They are out of line in more than one sense of the word.

At this point, when so many of us have so much opportunity, we need to be on our guard against adopting a victimhood narrative. In many parts of society today women are not victims unless we choose to be categorised as such. That description – and appropriate, urgent actions to help – should be reserved for those who are genuinely oppressed, disadvantaged or mistreated. Being the 'victim' of patronising language in the office is not comparable to the horrors of rape or modern slavery. A young girl reading all the media coverage about sexual harassment might well start to think that most men are predators, that serious assault is part of everyday working life today, that we have made no progress at all. We need to make the decision to be more empowered for the future than threatened by the past.

I'm not suggesting we gloss over terrible incidents – quite the opposite – but we need to take care over how we characterise things. As theatre director Emma Rice put it 'with a wry laugh' when asked about 'which #MeToo stories to tell': 'Me and my female friends – we are all replaying events that have happened in our past with a different lens.'

I found myself talking with a Jewish friend, around my age, about the dilemma over dredging up events of the past. The Brett Kavanaugh Supreme Court nomination hearings were in full, ugly flow as we spoke. My friend revealed he had experienced aggressive anti-Semitism as a teenager; in my early twenties I once fled a man's apartment – someone I had no reason to be wary of – fearing he was going to rape me. We compared notes; neither of us wanted to relive those difficult experiences by exposing the perpetrators three decades later. It helped that we were both confident that they were not engaging in such behaviours today. We agreed that sometimes the best way forward is to take the unfashionable route of forgiveness. I saw this when I reviewed progress in the Liberal Democrat Party eighteen months after my report; the procedures were in place to prevent future problems, but until someone decided to forgive, the hard feelings from the earlier issues continued to fester – and no one was a winner.

Of course, bad things *do* still happen. My advice to my children is to protect themselves wherever possible, and to speak up *immediately* if something inappropriate occurs. During his wedding speech, my son-in-law mentioned that for their first meeting, he'd invited Florence to his Paris hotel – 'and she absolutely refused', which made me smile.

In the aftermath of the furore around the men-only Presidents Club charity dinner, I admit to feeling quite disconcerted. My first reaction was incredulity that such blatant sexual harassment was openly occurring in 2018. Was the gap between what was being said and done really as great as the lurid accounts of that dinner suggested? The event was described as a 'City' dinner, yet I did not recognise the City I work in today from the reports. A 'round robin' email quickly revealed that many others (both men and women) felt the same – and wanted to do something to restore funds forfeited by the charities who now wanted nothing to do with the Presidents Club. So instead of feeling angry and helpless, we set up a new series of modern, inclusive fund-raising dinners, under the banner 'Diverse City'. The response has been overwhelmingly enthusiastic, with many people – including the Prime Minister – contacting me to say they love the idea of doing something positive in response to such a bad development. We're on track to replace all the funds lost, as well as to restore collective confidence that outlandish behaviour towards women is anomalous in our industry today.

What about 'everyday sexism' that can chip away at our confidence and morale? Most of us are not so fragile as to flounder at the smaller challenges, but we do need to work out a way through that doesn't just enable us to brush them off but prevent them from happening. People are usually mortified when they realise that their behaviour has undermined a colleague. A self-described 'alpha male' peer of mine put his head in his hands and apologised unreservedly when I told him (discreetly) that he had shaken a female colleague's confidence through his choice of words. Straight away he said, 'I was trying to help, but I get it, I messed up. How can I make amends?'

I can see now that throughout my life I have looked to engage with, rather than walk away from, those who have treated me with condescension. This hasn't necessarily been a conscious decision, but I have found it an effective approach. Richard tells me that it can be powerful to play the lower hand – the Iranian art of ta'arof: the etiquette of showing apparent humility or weakness while getting to know someone, and actually gaining the advantage in the process. A subtle, sophisticated – and successful – technique.

Meanwhile, we need to see the gender issue in the context of the whole of society, not as a separate topic. In America, progress for women has been uneven compared with other Western countries since the time when I was so dazzled at the start of my career by those glamorous colleagues in New York. Amazingly, when US voters went to the polls in November 2016 there was still no guaranteed paid maternity leave in America. (Only Oman and Papua New Guinea share this dubious distinction.) It would be ironic – but entirely welcome – if President Trump addressed this: encouraged by his daughter Ivanka, he has proposed guaranteeing six weeks of paid leave to families (including those who adopt). We also need to understand why 62% of non-college-educated white women and 45% of white college-educated women voted for Trump, and the reasons for their disaffection with status quo politics. We can help heal the divisions in society by listening to, not dismissing, other views. Yet so often, those who define themselves as liberal are quick to judge, rather than welcoming and respecting other opinions, especially those they see as less enlightened or modern. Illiberal liberalism is an easy contradiction to adopt without even noticing. If we really want to build bridges and make progress, we need to guard against any sense of superiority (wherever it emanates from) and seek to understand other perspectives. That includes studiously avoiding even the slightest implication that attaining gender equality involves pitting women against men – we are trying to move on from the past oppression of one sex, not repeat it.

Overt political correctness – and the inevitable backlashes – are further manifestations of a flawed, yet all-too-common divisive approach. It's easy to blame an over-zealous 'diversity agenda' (whether real or imaginary) for a whole host of developments. Lazy newspaper headlines like '"Big Four" arts bodies face cuts to funding in name of diversity' (*Daily Telegraph*, 28 June 2017) stir up negativity – in fact, that article reveals the largest UK arts companies agreed to take 'a hit for the greater good'. Arts Council chairman Sir Nicholas Serota explained: 'This is about national organisations recognising that they can only really flourish if the whole ecology flourishes.' A headline along the lines of '"Big Four" arts bodies share funding to support diverse artists' would have been a less sensational but more accurate version of events. And the stories keep coming, thick and fast: today's newspapers carry reports that an Oxford professor has launched legal action against the university because he was told he must retire to promote 'diversity and intergenerational fairness'. If true, the university would, of course, be promoting the *myth* of diversity and intergenerational fairness rather than the real thing. At this juncture, we have to stay vigilant about unhelpful accusations in 'the name of diversity'.

Which leads on to our second risk, that we focus too much on one side of the gender equality equation. To achieve widespread progression for women, men will need more choices too. And as we saw in Chapter 9, this does not just mean formal policies and procedures that theoretically enable men to be less 'alpha', but attitudes to match.

Instead of simplistic identity politics, we need to develop (and to keep reinforcing) a more sophisticated concept of diversity and inclusion that means just that, one that benefits everyone and improves our thinking. I've seen many glimpses of a more evolved approach, only to be followed by lapses back into the mindset that favours the unrepresented over 'the establishment'. The late Charles Krauthammer, a Pulitzer Prize-winning columnist, made the point provocatively when speaking of the lack of true diverse thinking at American universities: 'Stanford ... abandoned its "Western Civilization" course because of its bias toward white males (you know: narrow-minded ethnics like Socrates, Jesus and Jefferson).'

Identity politics are counterproductive when it comes to achieving our goal of true inclusion. In America, for example, we can see that tribalism is rife, and every group feels attacked to some extent – whites, blacks, hispanics, men and women. We urgently need to reclaim the diversity agenda before it takes on a meaning that is the exact opposite of what was originally intended, with counterproductive consequences like 'diversity fatigue', those eye-rolling moments and outright resentment.

The third risk on my list is that by emulating men rather than 'working' our difference we might – ironically – miss our moment. It's another insidious, easy-to-fall-into trap: after all, we've been accustomed to a certain definition of success for a very long time. As we explored earlier, we need to encourage creative girls to be creative, if that is where their talents lie, rather than pressuring them to study STEM subjects or become doctors or lawyers – unless that is really what they want to do. I am delighted that my youngest daughter spends her free time doing 'kitchen sink science' experiments and will obviously encourage her to progress right the way through to a career in scientific research if her passion continues, but when an older daughter struggled with Physics we were happy for her to drop it and take Spanish instead. She proved a natural, and ended up with an A* grade, at both GCSE and A level. A quick glance at students' A level choices shows persistent and significant preferences according to gender, that we should at least respect. It would be snatching defeat from the jaws of victory if at the very moment when difference is becoming prized, we do not encourage our daughters to pursue their genuine interests. It's hard to imagine what could be more important than creative, lateral thinking – especially when we are competing with artificial intelligence.

The fourth risk on my list is the 'first world problem' concern. A scarcity of women on boards or female CEOs cannot be compared with the dangers and difficulties faced by girls growing up in underprivileged areas in our own Western countries, as well as in parts of Asia, the Middle East, or Africa. I have personally wrestled with this, but have come to see that it's important to work on both ends of the spectrum of gender issues – and the middle, too. That doesn't mean the same person doing all that work. Think of our efforts as a patchwork quilt, coming together to create the whole.

The reality is I have been able to be much more effective by focusing on a specific area close to my experiences, than if I had vaguely championed women's interests. The narrow aim of the 30% Club has broadened, both geographically and along the career journey, and that evolution makes sense as the approach has proven effective. But if its original aim had encompassed 'schoolroom to boardroom' across the world, the 30% Club would have failed. As individuals, we can be more productive by being focused, but it takes numerous simultaneous efforts to form the powerful combination needed for broad progress. Working sequentially or solving just part of the issue or in one corner of the globe just won't get us there.

A brief look at the history of female progression shows a consistent pattern throughout the world. Of course that pattern is not predictable, and progress can be elliptical; today, for example, we see renewed need for protection against domestic violence in the UK. But the broad sweep of change follows similar steps:

Stage one: safety and protection from domestic violence

Stage two: access to education for girls

Stage three: civil rights – including claims to property and the right to vote

Stage four: equal opportunity for employment, then equal pay

Stage five: awareness that legislation isn't enough; efforts are needed to overcome covert discrimination and lingering prejudice

Stage six: realisation of the benefits of true balance, including the opportunity for both women and men to influence, to lead, to create, to participate, to work in partnership as equals – to have choices and to be fulfilled.

In 1943, psychologist Abraham Maslow famously developed 'A theory of human motivation' which he described as a hierarchy of needs, from basic physical requirements

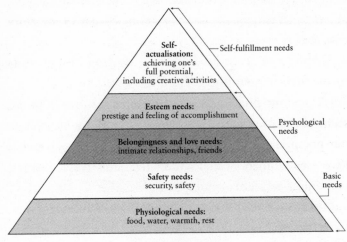

Maslow's Pyramid

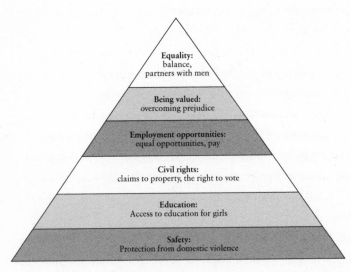

Women's Rights Pyramid

to 'self-actualisation' or personal growth. (He later expanded the five original stages to encompass eight, concluding with spiritual needs.)

The development of women's rights can be mapped on to a similar pyramid.

It's obviously hard to get to the pinnacle if we have not secured the foundation, but the basics alone understate our potential, as human beings and – in our new version here – as women. We shouldn't feel embarrassed about continuing to blaze a trail to the top; after all, I am who I am because of the women who preceded me. They undertook the much greater challenge of tackling the outright oppression of women and we can in turn 'pay it forward', helping the next generation to start even higher up the pyramid. But we should also be mindful that there are still very many women facing significant obstacles, including on our own doorstep. My current mentees, never complaining, always enthusiastic, and from very different ethnic groups to mine, constantly remind me of the need for this broader perspective.

One particular event captured, for me, the necessity of multiple efforts to help women progress around the world – and the far greater heroism of those involved in securing the basic safety of too many disadvantaged girls.

In 2014 I was invited to speak at the Milken Institute Global Conference in Los Angeles. I am intrinsically wary of big gatherings of the great and the good (I have never been to the World Economic Forum at Davos, for example) – I worry that they perpetuate 'the bubble'. Milken deliberately aims for an eclectic crowd of 'doers' – there are, for example, no keynote speeches – and the aim is to encourage collaboration to turn powerful ideas into even more powerful action. I decided to see for myself. The investor panel I participated in discussed putting 'money where our mouths are' and investing more in companies that were advancing diversity. Afterwards, the conference organisers got back in touch and told me that they wanted to back their words with deeds, and so would be targeting 30% female panellists for the 2015 conference. I returned the following year to find they had *almost* hit the goal (29%), and had managed to weave the topic of gender equality into three days of discussions covering everything from the environment to geopolitics to medical research.

The *pièce de résistance* was a lunchtime session, challenging the audience 'What would you do to make the world better for women and girls?'

The Milken team had assembled a diverse line-up of speakers: women and men who were all doing something quite distinct, each committed in their own way to making the world better for women and girls. Some were famous, others less so. They came from a wide range of countries and backgrounds. All had found their 'niche'. Actress Patricia Arquette spoke about the importance of equal pay: she had won the Academy Award for Best Supporting Actress just a couple of months earlier, and used her acceptance speech to demand pay equality for all American women. Her fellow Hollywood star, Freida Pinto, used her moment on the Milken stage to introduce the audience to

'Girl Rising India' – part of a global initiative to educate more girls. Dr Deborah Birx, US Global AIDS Coordinator, talked about the vulnerability of young girls in parts of Africa to HIV infection. Shiza Shahid, co-founder of the Malala Fund, spoke about the challenges faced by young women in Pakistan. Cherie Blair spoke about her Foundation and the importance of mentoring business-women in emerging and developing economies – and, as requested, I talked about the 30% Club.

There were eighteen speakers in all, and between us we covered everywhere from Saudi Arabia to America, from shanty towns to the boardroom. At the bottom of the pyramid, a long, long way to go before we could possibly say it's a good time to be a girl; at the top, the prospect of true equality coming ever more clearly into view.

We were hearing tales of extremes, but of course within every region, country, religion and culture there is also a very wide range of women's experiences. We are the *same but different*, the wonderful title of a Business in the Community photographic project celebrating diverse women. If each of us finds a specific area where we can help drive progress, all the while being aware of the bigger picture, we can amplify our individual efforts.

And those towards the top of the pyramid can have not just greater impact but wider appeal if they are mindful of that broader context. The #MeToo campaign went viral after Hollywood actress Alyssa Milano tweeted, 'If all the women who have been sexually harassed or assaulted wrote 'Me too' as a status, we might give people a sense of the magnitude of the problem'. Over the following 24 hours, 4.7 million people around the world engaged in the #MeToo conversation on Facebook alone, catalysing a shift in how this issue is seen. A testament to the power women can yield today.

But not all women. Unknown to Milano when she posted her tweet, the seeds of the #MeToo movement had been sown more than twenty years earlier when a 13-year-old girl confided in activist Tarana Burke that she was being sexually abused by her mother's boyfriend. Burke describes how she reacted at the time: 'I was horrified by her words, the emotions welling inside me ... I literally could not take it any more ... right in the middle of her sharing her pain with me I cut her off ... I watched her put her mask back on and go back into the world like she was all alone and I couldn't even bring myself to whisper ... me too.' This was the heartbreaking background to Burke's original campaign to help victims of sexual assault. Burke is black and much of her work is focused on empowering young black girls. She notes (without resentment) that it wasn't until famous – and white – women got involved that the profile of her long-running campaign soared. The impact of Milano's tweet highlights both the opportunity that comes with being at the pinnacle of the pyramid – and the responsibility. Being aware of this privileged position, reaching back and across wherever we can, will help deliver progress for more women across the world and garner support to tackle our own remaining obstacles.

At a dinner to celebrate the publication of *The Female Lead*, a compilation of stories and photos of sixty 'women who shape our world', the brainchild of entrepreneur Edwina Dunn, the conversation oscillated between enormous optimism and varying degrees of despondency. One of the most impressive and moving stories was shared by Nimco Ali, FGM survivor and now activist, who showed how she looks forwards and protects her nieces from the risk of FGM rather than dwells on her own pain. Nimco and I have since followed up to consider how we could combine our different experiences, contacts, expertise and even 'brands'. A goal of 30% reduction in global FGM, accompanied by a programme to invest in girls' education championed by influential men would bring together our different 'specialist subjects' and potentially make far greater impact than either of us could on our own. We cannot change the past but – together – we can write the future.

Which leads on to our fifth, most daunting challenge – the real danger of a backlash against diversity and inclusion as a consequence of ill-thought-through immigration policies, fears over Islamic extremism and more general economic disparities and social exclusion. If welcoming others makes us vulnerable, if progress for one group is seen as being at the expense of incumbents, it would hardly be surprising to see less enthusiasm for inclusion.

As we've explored throughout this book, there's a great deal of inconsistent – if not completely contradictory – thinking around diversity today. We need to step back and reconsider the concepts of inclusion, balance and tolerance.

Let's be clear: respecting a wide range of views is *not* synonymous with 'anything goes', especially where that 'anything' involves harming others. We embrace a wide range of sexual orientations and gender identities, but that does not mean paedophilia is acceptable. We can and must have boundaries, and that does not make us intolerant. So when it comes to the challenge of violent and extreme forms of Islam, for example, it would be hopelessly muddled to conflate the respecting of different religions with tolerating ideology aimed at destruction. To avoid a backlash, we need to constantly distinguish between radicalism and the views of many Muslims, who are appalled by the violence and who reject the extremist ideology. Criticising radical Islamism – the ideology that seeks to impose a radical reading of Islam on society, often by violent means – should not be seen as incompatible with welcoming religious diversity and respecting the faith of Muslims.

You may think I have only one answer for everything (in my defence, it's the one solution that hasn't really been tried before), but here, as in so many other situations, I believe that women hold the key to tackling the threat. Activist Maria Munir explains how Muslim women and young people 'are active participants in the reclamation of religion from people who use it to promote violence based on toxic masculinity'. Munir presses for more recognition that Islamic communities are very diverse in themselves and for a better understanding of women within these communities. Muslim women are not 'solely victims of gendered violence, we also fight to stop it, by challenging outdated preachers and reviving new techniques of engaging with maligned people'. Former chief executive of the UK Association of Police and Crime Commissioners Nazir Afzal agrees; he suggests that to find solutions we 'don't concentrate on the community leaders, we find the new community stars ... more than half the Muslims in [the UK] are under 25, female and from low-income backgrounds. The leaders are male middle-class professionals. They have no idea what is going on in their own families, never mind the wider communities. We should move away from these people and go to the women's groups who are tackling radicalisation, sexual abuse and other issues in communities and they are doing it really, really well.'

In the UK, examples of groups tackling radicalisation and extremism include Inspire, founded in 2008 by human rights campaigner Sara Khan, and WARN (Women Against Radicalisation Network), set up by Henna Rai in 2015. Khan has recognised the important role that Muslim mothers in particular can play in the battle against the radicalisation of young people. Inspire runs workshops 'equipping mothers with theological counter-narratives so that they could feel more confident about challenging their children's views within the home'. Similarly, Henna Rai's organisation WARN runs workshops for Muslim girls and women to help them to challenge gender discrimination and practices such as forced marriage and FGM, drawing on feminist readings of the Qur'an as well as human rights law. Globally, organisations like Musawah (Arabic for 'equality'), a movement launched in 2009 in Kuala Lumpur, are working for justice and equality in the family and wider society, again based on both a feminist interpretation of the Qur'an and on international human rights standards. Most famously, one of the bravest stands against Islamic extremism was taken by schoolgirl Malala Yousafzai, who, after being shot by the Taliban at the age of 15 as punishment for her advocacy for girls' education, established the Malala Fund to promote girls' education in countries with large Muslim populations.

'Islamic women for peace' is, like the other ambitions outlined in this book, not a naïve dream, but actually happening today. By giving greater exposure and support to women like Sara Khan and Henna Rai, non-Muslims can help create a snowball effect, encouraging more Muslim women and girls to lend their voices to the struggle against extremism. The more we begin to see these women – not radical preachers – as representatives of Islam and Muslim communities, the less likelihood that there will be a backlash against religious tolerance.

This is a process that Muslim men can support without fear of losing out themselves. There is historical precedent, particularly in the Arab world. In the nineteenth and twentieth centuries, Egyptians Rifa'a Rafi' Tahtawi and Qasim Amin and Tunisians Tahar Haddad and Hassan Hosni Abdelwaheb played pioneering roles in the struggle for girls' education. Contemporary Muslim men who wish to challenge the narratives of Islamic extremism can follow their example.

Of course, all of this will not be easy. Of the roughly 800 million Muslim women in the world, many do not have the necessary economic, social and political capital to effect meaningful change. In Iran, women make up less than 20% of the workforce even though over 50% of university graduates are women. In the UK, Muslim women are three times as likely as women in general to be unemployed, due to a combination of family pressures, prejudice and discrimination, poverty and language barriers. The obstacles are real, but we can help through practical steps including inclusive hiring practices. Meanwhile, uninformed impressions that Islamic women are universally oppressed are far from accurate. It's a long way from Morocco to Malaysia, both geographically and culturally. Prior to the 2017 UK general election, five Muslim-majority countries had more women in parliament than the UK (Senegal, Algeria, Tunisia, Sudan and Iraq). There is even a thriving 30% Club in the Gulf Co-Operation Countries.

We must seek a solution to the scourge of Islamic extremism, which has not only caused death and fearfulness but threatens religious tolerance and broader progress towards a more diverse and inclusive society. As in so many other controversial areas – transgenderism, for example – we need empathetic thinking. Balancing different interests – LGBTQ and religious beliefs, for example – is incredibly difficult, requiring sensitivity and thoughtfulness, not dogma or the pretence of certainty. Sometimes, we need to agree to disagree, to learn to respect another's point of view.

Over the past few years, another very big theme has been the rise in 'populism', linked to globalisation, economic injustice and social exclusion. As income and wealth inequality has increased, so the melting pot has become overheated. I strongly believe this is largely attributable to remote policy-making, and certainly not to 'too much' diversity. We desperately need genuine diversity of thought if we are to achieve anything approaching broad economic prosperity and to heal the deep divisions.

Again, this is not wishful thinking. Over the past two years, I have served as one of 22 'Commissioners' working with the Institute for Public Policy Research on a new model for longer-term growth and a fairer UK economy. The group was certainly an eclectic bunch: 11 men and 11 women, with the youngest member in her twenties and the eldest in his seventies, and wide-ranging ethnic backgrounds, roles and experiences. It included the Archbishop of Canterbury, the co-founder of artificial intelligence company DeepMind and the general secretary of the British Trades Union Congress. It was fascinating and encouraging to see how our diverse perspectives converged on some really quite radical ideas. For example, we advocated increased minimum wages to improve productivity, agreeing that people are more engaged if they feel valued. The conventional thinking is that businesses need better productivity to justify pay rises. Many argued that our recommendations were unworkable, but less than a month after we published our report, Amazon increased wages significantly for 17,000 UK workers. I've seen time and again that diverse, honest thinking focused on tangible actions is not just possible, but can really yield results.

If we are to thrive, we certainly need to involve more women in the global workplace. McKinsey estimates that US$28 trillion could be added to the worldwide economy by 2025 if women were to be equal participants in the labour force with men. Japan is an obvious example of a country where unlocking female potential is a vital part of the solution to the economic challenges of its rapidly ageing population. (Shockingly, but graphically, sales of infant nappies are lower than sales of adult nappies in Japan.)

The challenges are different in each country but technology is creating visibility and shared knowledge. The international chapters of the 30% Club (there are now ten) have all taken the same core approach: engaging senior male business leaders, setting measurable, voluntary targets, working collaboratively and, ideally, with government support. The network is global, but local passion, leadership and knowledge are key: each 30% Club is adapted to suit a distinct culture and to address specific issues. In my view, change must not be imposed by outsiders, as that can encourage people to be defensive or even reactionary. Change needs to emanate from a genuine recognition of the economic and social benefits of diversity and equality within a country. We can share learning, but *who are we to tell other people what to do?*

I believe we should be more optimistic than ever before that *this time is different*, that we should consciously decide to overcome the remaining challenges to create balance so that there is not even an implicit sense that one half of humanity is superior to the other: this, in turn, will make us more likely to welcome and respect all 'others', to be less aggressive and longer term in our thinking. That seems a good incentive to really finish the task.

As a fund manager, I have been trained to be nervous about claims that 'this time is different'. There have been so many attempts before now to achieve radical change in the balance of power between men and women. Opportunity Now, Business in the Community's gender equality campaign, was originally called Opportunity 2000 at its launch in October 1991 (the month I first became a mother and became all too aware of the gender problem at work). It was all supposed to be fixed by the year 2000. In recent years the conversation around women in the workplace has been deafening, yet as we've explored, *still* there are many unresolved issues.

None of this should divert our attention from what lies ahead if we choose. Periodic episodes of great progress have been seen over the past two centuries; the efforts – and results – have come in waves rather than being consistent. The history of feminism in Europe and North America is often described in terms of those waves – the first being the suffrage movements of the nineteenth and early twentieth century, the second the 'Women's Lib' movement of the 1960s and 1970s, and the third the recent expansion of this second wave, picking up where that left off and being more inclusive. These efforts have been part of a big build-up to this moment when it's not about women adapting to the male environment, but about creating a new environment with men. This wave is potentially unstoppable for it involves all of us – it is not 'top down', not about adding a few more women to existing structures but creating new ways of working, living and doing business that suit modern men as well as women.

Let's just remind ourselves of the enormity of the multiple, compounding factors that give us this breakthrough moment. The technology that flattens power structures and changes the nature of effective leadership; the dislocations that demand new thinking and place a premium on feminine behaviours; the 'coming of age' of diversity to mean diversity of thought, the ability to solve problems. These are the preconditions; our children who are growing up in this time of great change can help us turn the opportunity into reality – boys and girls who are being educated using technology, who socialise and influence through the internet and expect to make their impact any time, any place, anywhere in the world. Who see work as an activity, not a place, their sisters and brothers as equals, and who expect that great odyssey, not just a career. But they cannot do it alone. They need parents, teachers, mentors, employers, CEOs and politicians to help champion the big rebalance. To create a new narrative that is both more ambitious and much more subtle and sophisticated than helping women fit into the old one. A goal that doesn't require a campaign but a different way of thinking.

All of us have a part to play in making it not just a good time to be a girl but a better time for everyone.

Afterword

This is your time
This is your dance
Make every moment
Leave nothing to chance …

MICHAEL W. SMITH

One of the poignant aspects of being a (serial) mother is the constant stream of reminders about the circle of life. Over the past year, both Fitz and Florence have got married. Florence and her husband Benjamin have a beautiful baby boy, Julian, so Richard and I have been learning all over again as we take on new roles as first-time grandparents. Millie has joined her two brothers at Oxford University. Clara decided to do a foundation art course, deferring her university place. She did brilliantly in her A levels, helping to build her confidence. Theo and Cecily have just moved up to senior school. Tuppy is off on a year abroad, as part of his modern languages course. Oki is about to embark on her GCSE exams. Bea is more into her science experiments than ever before. On a personal level, it's an exciting – and emotional – time, seeing the next generation's expectations, anxieties, hopes and dreams unfold.

As we've explored throughout this book, I am optimistic about my children's future but also mindful of the many siren voices that may undermine their confidence and, ultimately, their happiness. These are the essential pieces of advice I repeat to them – and to you:

Leap before you look. Be open to possibilities, willing to explore and bold in your ambition. Push out your boundaries, if only gradually. You may well be surprised by just how much you can achieve.

Think big, start small, but start now. There are always reasons not to do something. If you have an idea, don't let the fear of what might go wrong stop you from trying – and don't think you need to map out every step of the way in advance. Focus on your vision, not a spreadsheet.

Own the process. Play to your strengths – don't submerge the differences that define you. This is your life: feeling happy and fulfilled is an absolute not a relative game. Recognise when you feel most content and build on those moments.

Act as confidently as you can – people have confidence in confident people. Try to remember that everyone has insecurities. Devise techniques to help you until you actually become confident.

Setbacks are inevitable. What matters is how you respond to them. Every career – every life – is a labyrinth, not a ladder.

Ask for help – none of us has all the answers. It's a sign of strength – not weakness – to seek advice. Find friends who genuinely want you to succeed, look for a partner in life as well as in love.

Help others where you can – it's very empowering, as well as a good thing to do. Be aware of others and if you see someone who needs help, don't leave it to someone else: offer your assistance. Pay it forward. You can play your part in making true gender equality a reality.

If you want to be a CEO, go for it. And do it in your own, authentic way. Whether or not you aspire to be a CEO, look to take control of your destiny.

Remember there is no one single 'right' path, no formula for success, no rulebook about family and/ or career. Check in with yourself every now and again – has what's important to you changed? What version of your future self would make you feel happy? Whatever scenario you envisage, make sure you can provide for yourself.

It's a good time to be a girl – but it's not all sorted yet. If you are bullied or harassed, speak up – you will be heard. If your environment is discouraging, your priority is to find a new one. If the first route doesn't work out, the second may well do (remember my own contrasting early career experiences).

Most of all, remember that this is your time.

WE ARE ALL WONDERWOMEN!
★

Notes

Preface

4   capital firms' investments: 'Venture Capital's Funding
     Gender Gap is Actually Getting Worse', Valentina Zaria,
     based on Pitchbook data, *Fortune*, 14 March 2017. The
     evidence suggests that growing numbers of women are
     starting businesses, 'Surge in female entrepreneurs narrows
     UK gender gap', Andy Bounds, *Financial Times*, 4 July
     2017, but many are unable or unwilling to scale up their
     small enterprises.

8   treated every hour: Plan International UK, April 2017
     report based on data released by NHS Digital, covering the
     period from April 2015 to March 2016: https://plan-uk.org/
     media-centre/fgm-identified-in-medical-appointments-
     every-hour-on-average-stats-show.

8   record high in 2017: 'Child trafficking in UK hits a record
     high, figures show', *The Independent*, April 2017, statistics
     published by the UK Government's National Referral
     Mechanism.

8   of any group: 'Class Differences: Ethnicity and
    Disadvantage', Carl Cullinane and Philip Kirby, The Sutton
    Trust, November 2016.

Chapter 1: A tale of two career women

23 less than men: 'Cracking the Code', 30% Club research
    conducted by YSC and KPMG, 2014, p. 10.

Who received 5 or more promotions?

🧍	65%	74%
🧍	51%	57%

23 took part in Project 28–40: https://gender.bitc.org.uk/
    all-resources/research-articles/project-28-40-report.
24 Perhaps unsurprisingly: 'Junior lawyers are failing to hit
    billing targets', Thomas Connelly, *Legal Cheek*, 24 October
    2016, based on data in PwC 25th Annual Law Firms Survey
    2016.

Chapter 2: New leadership required

40 we were 'antifragile': Antifragility is a concept developed by
    Nassim Nicholas Taleb in *Antifragile: Things that Gain
    from Disorder,* first published in 2012 by Random House.
    In the book's prologue, Taleb defines antifragility as 'beyond
    resilience or robustness. The resilient resists shocks and
    stays the same; the antifragile gets better. This property is

behind everything that has changed with time: evolution, culture, ideas, revolutions, political systems, technological innovations, cultural and economic success, corporate survival, good recipes (say, chicken soup or steak tartare with a drop of cognac), the rise of cities, cultures, legal systems, bacterial resistance ... even our own existence as a species on this planet.' Taleb goes on to emphasise, 'Antifragility has a singular property of allowing us to deal with the unknown, to do things without understanding them – and do them well.'

42 he connected with them: Trump did not win a popular majority but did enough in the neglected middle states of America to win the all-important electoral college majority. https://theconversation.com/us-election-final-results-how-trump-won-69356.

43 through one or more shared board members: Source: Simon Kuestenmacher, geographer and demographer at The Demographics Group, Melbourne, Australia.

44 55% of the total: Source: Autonomous Research, Bloomberg.

44 'won retail': 'How Amazon Won Retail in One Chart (With Or Without Whole Foods)', John Koetsier, Inc.com, 23 June 2017.

Chapter 3: The 30% Club: the strength of feminine power

50 literature I was reading: For example, 'Critical Mass Theory and Women's Political Representation', Sarah Childs, University of Bristol and Mona Lena Krook, Washington University in St Louis, 2007.

51 René Obermann: 'Deutsche Telekom sets 30% female quota', *gtb* (Global Telecoms Business), 15 March 2010.

53 what went wrong: *Rogers Commission Report*, submitted to President Ronald Reagan on 9 June 1986.

53 'the great and the good': 'Gone by the board? Why bank directors did not spot credit risks', Francesco Guerrera, *Financial Times*, 25 June 2008.

54 all-male boards: 'Improving the Gender Balance on British Boards', *Women on Boards. Davies Review*, Five Year Summary October 2015.

65 directors to date: http://www.boardsforum.co.uk/ alumnaeappointments as at September 2018.

65 Committee members: Initially, the 30% Club Steering Committee comprised senior, influential women, but of course a key 30% Club principle is collaboration with men, so today the group is more diverse, including men and those at an earlier stage of their careers. Everyone is a 'doer' – leading or involved in a specific aspect of the 30% Club's work. The original members who remain involved are: Gaenor Bagley (PwC), Tamara Box (Reed Smith), Caroline Carr (Permira), Gay Collins (Montfort Communications), Melanie Gee (Lazard), Mary Goudie (Labour peer), Vimi Grewal-Carr (Deloitte), Emma Howard Boyd (ShareAction), Professor Heather McGregor (Edinburgh Business School), Melanie Richards (KPMG), Henrietta Royle (British Bankers' Association), Joanna Santinon (EY), Jane Scott (The Professional Boards Forum), Sian Westerman (Rothschild), Sarah Wiggins (Linklaters) and Diana Brightmore-Armour (ANZ). Brenda Trenowden (ANZ) took over from me as chair of the committee in 2015, supported by Emily Lawson as deputy chair. Others who joined later and have made a big impact include Karin Barnick (Korn Ferry), Jamie Brookes (RBS), Pavita Cooper (More Difference), Liz Dimmock (Women Ahead), Mary Fitzpatrick (GE), Deborah Gilshan (Aberdeen Standard Investments), Katushka Giltsoff (The Miles Partnership), Claudia Harris (Careers and Enterprise UK), Nick Jarman

(PwC), Avril Martindale (Freshfields), Elizabeth Passey
(non-executive director), Anne Richards (M&G), Rachel
Short (Where Women Work). A special mention must go to
Claudia Kohler and Francoise Higson, project managers for
the 30% Club, for their tireless efforts over many years and
to Niamh Corbett of Board Intelligence, the first 'millennial'
steering committee member, for her generous and
thoughtful advice.

66   money changing hands: There has never been a 30% Club
membership fee; individual volunteers give their time,
companies donate resources, including venues for events,
and if they join the cross-company mentoring programme
pay a small charge to cover the costs of running the scheme,
including software to match pairs and avoid conflicts of
interest.

68   'When Woman is Boss': 'When Woman is Boss', an
interview with Nikola Tesla by John B. Kennedy, *Collier's*
magazine, 30 January 1926.

Chapter 4: Men, women, equal, different

74   much the same: In 2017, boys slightly outperformed girls at
A levels, with 26.6% of boys achieving an A* or A grade,
compared with 26.1% of girls. This was the first time boys
had outperformed girls in seventeen years, although the gap
had been narrowing, with girls just 0.3 percentage points
ahead of boys in 2016 at the top two grades. In 2018, boys
again slightly outperformed girls (26.6% A*/A compared
with 26.2% of girls).

78   'in the first place': Interview with Debra W. Soh, Sex
Neuroscientist, Claire Lehmann, Quillette.com, 20 January
2017.

79   gender stereotyping: 'Sex differences in human neonatal
social perception', Jennifer Connellan, Simon Baron-Cohen,

et al., *Infant Behavior and Development*, Volume 23, Issue 1, January 2000, pages 113–18.

80 'Reading the Mind in the Eyes' test: The '"Reading the Mind in the Eyes" Test Revised Version (2001): A Study with Normal Adults, and Adults with Asperger Syndrome or High-functioning Autism', Simon Baron-Cohen, Sally Wheelwright, Jacqueline Hill, Yogini Raste and Ian Plumb, University of Cambridge. The test is available to take online at http://socialintelligence.labinthewild.org/mite/

80 'Google's Ideological Echo Chamber': https://assets. documentcloud.org/documents/3914586/Googles-Ideological-Echo-Chamber.pdf

80 'there's more work to be done': https://www.google.com/ diversity/

82 STEM: Science, technology, engineering and maths.

83 'cultures and decades': www.heterodoxacademy.org: 'The Most Authoritative Review Paper on Gender Differences', Sean Stevens, 25 August 2017.

84 'You think you're infallible': http://www.wired.co.uk/article/ why-men-risk-it-all.

86 managers are women: https://group.tilney.co.uk/press/ articles/latest-study-reveals-increase-in-female-fund-managers-but-still-only-1-in-10-money-managers-are-women, 14 June 2017.

86 Aviva Investors: 'Fund managers disappoint over female hiring', Chris Newlands, *Financial Times*, 30 April 2017.

87 'Common Stock Investment': 'Boys will be Boys: Gender, Overconfidence, and Common Stock Investment', Brad M. Barber and Terrance Odean, *The Quarterly Journal of Economics*, Volume 116, Issue 1, 1 February 2001, pp. 261–92.

87 Other studies and data: For example, BlackRock blog, 'Men vs Women: The Confidence Gap', 23 December 2013 and

'Women, Money and their Alarming Lack of Confidence', Elizabeth Harris, *Forbes*, 29 September 2015. UK data also suggests that women's lack of confidence impacts their willingness to invest: a 2017 survey conducted by Boring Money revealed that only 10% of women have a stocks and shares ISA (a tax-free account for savings or investments) compared with 17% of men. 'Why do so few women invest', Laura Suter, *The Telegraph*, 23 May 2017, cites research from investment firm Fidelity: 'More than a third of the women who took part in the study said they did not feel confident investing, compared with 26% of men. More women also said they didn't have sufficient knowledge to invest and that they did not understand the stock market.'

89 collective intelligence of groups: https://www.researchgate.net/publication/51453001_What_makes_a_team_smarter_More_women.

90 across the globe: McKinsey: *Women Matter: Gender Diversity a Corporate Performance Driver*, October 2007. Credit Suisse Research Institute: *CS Gender 3000*, 'The Reward for Change', 22 September 2016. 'Women on Boards and Firm Financial Performance: A Meta-Analysis', Corinne Post and Kris Byron, 5 November 2014 and Société Générale: 'Getting the Right Women on Board', October 2011.

91 improves performance: 'Does Gender Diversity on Board Really Boost Company Performance?' Katherine Klein, Professor of Management at the Wharton School at the University of Pennsylvania, 18 May 2017.

94 one seminar: The event was based around the publication of the Valuing Your Talent Research Report, *Investing for Sustainable Growth*, January 2015.

95 business is concerned: 'Without Honour', Martin Vander Weyer, *The Spectator*, 24 June 2017.

97   pay rises and promotions: https://hbr.org/2014/06/
        why-women-dont-negotiate-their-job-offers.

Chapter 5: Diversity of thought: welcome until anyone disagrees!

102   'social identity': 'The social identity theory of intergroup
        behaviour', H. Tajfel and J.C. Turner, in *Psychology of
        Intergroup Relations*, ed. William G. Austin and Stephen
        Worchel, 2nd edn, 1986 [1979], pp. 7–24, Chicago: Nelson-
        Hall. For a clear summary of the theory, see https://www.
        simplypsychology.org/social-identity-theory.html.

108   was announced: *Evening Standard* front page, 11 May
        2017: 'London doctors on brink of creating first early
        warning system for four women's cancers'.

Chapter 6: Why CEOs need to rethink diversity

113   'equal billing': Dr Scott E. Page comments taken from *The
        Difference: how the Power of Diversity Creates Better
        Groups, Firms, Schools, and Societies*, Princeton University
        Press, 2008, his paper 'Making the Difference: Applying a
        Logic of Diversity', published in the Academy of
        Management Perspectives, November 2007 and an
        interview in the *New York Times*, 'In Professor's Model,
        Diversity = Productivity' with Claudia Dreifus, 8 January
        2008.

115   every good intention: *WIRED*: 'Facebook Publishes its
        Managing Bias Course for All', 28 August 2015.

116   'Why Diversity Programs Fail': 'Why Diversity Programs
        Fail', *Harvard Business Review* July–August 2016 issue.

118   *Thinking, Fast and Slow: Thinking, Fast and Slow*, Daniel
        Kahneman, Penguin, first published 2011.

118   'Gender Equality by Design': *What Works: Gender
        Equality by Design*, Iris Bohnet, Harvard University Press,
        2016.

129 In his speech: www.bankofengland.co.uk/publications: 'The Sneetches', speech by Andy Haldane, 13 May 2016.

134 mentoring experience: 30% Club Cross-Company Mentoring Scheme Information Pack 2017.

138 for the 30% Club: *Shifting the Needle: Increasing the Number of Women in UK Partnerships*, December 2012.

140 review in 2015: The Needle Starts to Shift, involving 20 firms and 900 professionals, December 2015.

140 40% in 2017: Norton Rose Fulbright, global partnership appointments April 2017, source: *Law Society Gazette*.

140 Citywire analyses the numbers: Citywire, an online publishing and information provider, analyses the prevalence of women on the front line of asset management in its Alpha Female study. The 2018 report reveals: 'Mixed gender teams produce better returns'.

143 there are just three today: there have been only fourteen black male CEOs in the entire history of the Fortune 500, three of whom are currently in position: Roger Ferguson at TIAA, Kenneth Frazier at Merck and Marvin Ellison at J.C. Penney.

145 a new list of 'HERoes': the *Financial Times* published the first HERoes list on 27 September 2017. Suki and I worked closely with Carola Hoyos, then Editor, Executive Appointments, and Editor, FT Non-Executive Directors' Club to get the list off the ground.

146 In a 2017 interview: 'Mary Portas: Why is it taboo to talk about what we earn?' Margarette Driscoll, *The Telegraph*, 19 November 2016.

147 Netflix 'leapfrogs Disney': 'Netflix Investors Wobble Over Growth Fears', Joseph Archer, *The Telegraph*, 15 July 2018.

Chapter 7: Own the process

154   a wonderful essay: 'Warren Buffett is bullish ... on women', Warren Buffett, *Fortune* magazine 2 May 2013.

157   Amy Cuddy gave: 'Your body language may shape who you are', Amy Cuddy, *TED.com*, 1 October 2012.

160   wonderful 100th anniversary event: NFWI Centenary Annual Meeting at the Royal Albert Hall, 4 June 2015.

161   In a radio interview: Sir Paul McCartney Reveals John Lennon's Insecurities, radiox.co.uk 18 October 2013.

166   a real problem in the UK: 'UK childcare is the most expensive in the world', *Daily Mail*, October 2016. Opportunity Project 28–40 found that one in five mothers had left work because their childcare costs were too high.

167   an independent review: Independent Review into Processes and Culture of the Liberal Democrats, Helena Morrissey, June 2013.

171   a pilot study at Cambridge University: 30% Club Student Aspiration Survey, March 2015, in association with KPMG.

171   we extended the study: the broader 30% Club study was named the Think Future Study April 2016, also conducted in association with KPMG.

172   less than half: Opportunity Now Project 28–40, p. 20.

185   'because they were women': 'Feisty dame who blazed a trail to the top', Margareta Pagano, *The Independent*, 3 October 2012.

187   around 2% of eligible couples: https://www.gov.uk/government/news/new-share-the-joy-campaign-promotes-shared-parental-leave-rights-for-parents, 12 February 2018.

Chapter 8: Camp CEO

194   *Cracking the Code*: research conducted by YSC in collaboration with KPMG for the 30% Club on a gender-intelligent approach to developing male and female corporate leaders, 10 December 2013.

200   More than two-thirds: 'Career or motherhood? For most women, it's still a drastic choice', Helena Morrissey, *The Telegraph*, 9 December 2013, citing interim findings from Project 28–40. The first 15,000 responses revealed that 71 per cent of women feel very conflicted between career aspirations and family responsibilities: 69 per cent of women said they feel society expects them to put family first and yet 62 per cent of women feel pressured to succeed both at home and at work.

Chapter 9: Gender equality: good news for men and boys too

223   'less of a man': 'More than half of men to have taken Shared Parental Leave think those who do it risk being seen as "less of a man"', Sam Dean, *The Telegraph*, 16 November 2016.

Chapter 10: Women, money and power

235   regular household spending: The proportion of household spending controlled by women is often cited as being around 80%, but there is little data to substantiate this, partly because much of the spending is accounted to married couples rather than to one or other partner.

238   many marketing professionals are women: Axonn Media's Gender in Marketing 2017 survey was completed by 288 respondents (59% women, 41% men). https://www.axonn.media/gender-in-marketing-2017. In the US, the *Boston Globe* published the percentage of women and men in each profession (data as of 2016): 55% of market research analysts and marketing specialists are women, as are 56.5% of advertising and promotions managers. Matt Rocheleau, 7 March 2017. https://www.bostonglobe.com/metro/2017/03/06/chart-the-percentage-women-and-men-each-profession/GBX22YsWl0XaeHghwXfE4H/story.html

246 limited by time, resources and competing priorities: The Money Charity conducted a study into the effectiveness of the new financial education programme in 2016, and headlined the report: 'Financial education in schools: how to fix two lost years?'

249 'ten years before them': Resolution Foundation, 'A New Generational Contract: The final report of the Intergenerational Commission', 8 May 2018. https://www. resolutionfoundation.org/advanced/a-new-generational-contract/

249 to keep up with their friends: Credit Karma/Qualtrics survey of over 1,000 US adults. 'Nearly 40% of millennials overspend to keep up with friends'. Tim Devaney, 30 May 2018. https://www.creditkarma.com/insights/i/ fomo-spending-affects-one-in-four-millennials/

249 'I Want to Be Rich and I'm Not Sorry': Jessica Knoll, *New York Times*, 28 April 2018

250 over the past two decades: this compares with the overall national growth rate of 44% for all businesses, according to the 2017 State of Women-Owned Businesses Report commissioned by American Express. https://about. americanexpress.com/sites/americanexpress.newshq. businesswire.com/files/doc_library/file/2017_SWOB_ Report_-FINAL.pdf

250 The statistics are stark: 'Funding for Female Entrepreneurs in the UK Takes a Tumble', David Prosser, 20 March 2018, Forbes. https://www.forbes.com/sites/davidprosser/2018/03/ 20/funding-for-female-entrepreneurs-in-the-uk-takes-a-tumble/#5e634306a93e

251 A poll conducted for the *Telegraph*'s excellent Women Mean Business campaign: 'Two thirds of British female business owners say they are still not taken seriously by investors, *Telegraph* poll reveals' by Eleanor Steafel, Ashley

Kirk and Claire Cohen, 8 March 2018. https://www.
telegraph.co.uk/women/business/two-thirds-british-
female-business-owners-say-still-not-taken/

251   same level of financial backing: 'Why Women-Owned
Startups Are a Better Bet', Katie Abouzahr, Frances Brooks
Taplett, Matt Krentz and John Harthorne, 6 June 2018,
Boston Consulting Group. https://www.bcg.com/en-gb/
publications/2018/why-women-owned-startups-are-better-
bet.aspx

Chapter 11: We can write the future together

256   'with a different lens': 'Personally I Can't Jump on the
#MeToo Bandwagon', Claire Allfree, *The Telegraph*, 11
October 2018.

261   'Socrates, Jesus and Jefferson': 'The Tribalization of America',
Charles Krauthammer, *Washington Post*, 6 August 1990.

261   A quick glance: http://www.telegraph.co.uk/
education/2016/08/18/a-level-results-2016-which-subjects-
did-students-do-the-best-and/. Gender gap: the subjects with
the biggest gender divides.

Gender gap: the A-level subjects with the biggest gender divides
Subjects that girls prefer

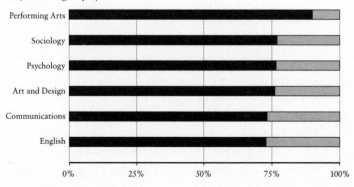

Subjects that boys prefer

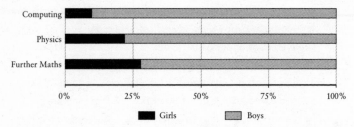

271 ‘they are doing it really, really well’: ‘ISIS is effectively a gang and being part of a gang is a thrill’: Why some people become radicalised, Nazir Afzal, *The Mirror*, 5 June 2017.

271 ‘equipping mothers’: *The Battle for British Islam*, Sara Khan, Saqi Books, 2016, p. 180.

275 McKinsey estimates: *The Power of Parity*, McKinsey Global Institute, September 2015, p. 8, the ‘full potential’ scenario.

275 sales of infant nappies: ‘There are more adult diapers sold in Japan than baby diapers’, Sally Herships, Marketplace. org, 29 August 2016

Acknowledgements

I am grateful to so many people who have helped me to write this book by sharing their thoughts and experiences.

I am indebted to those who have taken a chance on me at critical moments, who listened and gave their advice freely. To my parents and sister Liz, who made it a good time to be this particular girl when I was growing up. Thank you to Donald Cameron, for that very first vote of confidence in offering me a job at Schroders, to Stewart Newton and my former colleagues at Newton and BNY Mellon – in particular Ron O'Hanley, Curtis Arledge and Michael Cole-Fontayn – for giving me the chances to leap before I looked! Thank you to the five enlightened Chairmen who formed the 30% Club Advisory Council and demonstrated how much can be achieved by men and women working together: Sir Roger Carr, Sir Win Bischoff, Robert Swannell, Glen Moreno and David Cruickshank.

Thank you to Peter Grauer for immediately saying 'yes' when I asked him to lead the US 30% Club – even though he hardly knew me at the time – and to Nigel Wilson at Legal and General for his counsel and vision.

Special thanks are due to the 30% Club Steering Committee members – in particular Baroness Goudie, Melanie Richards and Brenda Trenowden, and all those companies and chairmen who didn't extrapolate the past or say 'no' but looked forward and created the change we all wanted.

I'd like to pay tribute to Niamh Corbett, who was such a thoughtful sounding board in the early stages of this book, to Sir Roger Carr and Mark Zinkula for their valuable feedback on early drafts, to all my wonderful children for being so willing to contribute as well as to bear with me when I was writing, and of course to Richard, for sharing his valuable perspective, for reading and re-reading the material and – most importantly! – for his unconditional love.

And finally, a huge thank you to my agent Georgina Capel, who wrote back to me within five minutes of my asking if she might be willing to represent me, and to Arabella Pike of William Collins and her wonderful team who enabled an idea to become a reality.

Index